SCHOLASTIC

ALPHA Grammar and Composition

3

Vaishali Batra
Series editor: Anne Seaton

About ALPHA™ Grammar and Composition

Welcome to **Scholastic ALPHA™ Grammar and Composition.**

This series comprises coursebooks for classes 1 to 5 and offers an easy, engaging and meaningful way to master the skills and mechanics of English **Grammar**, **Composition** and **Comprehension**.

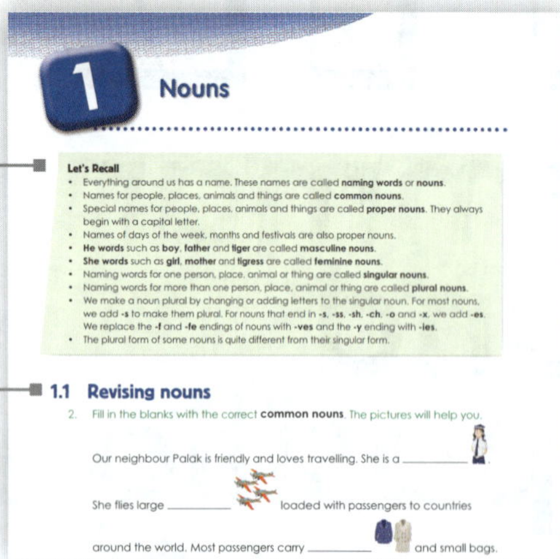

Easy recall of prior topic followed by an exercise to check for readiness to learn

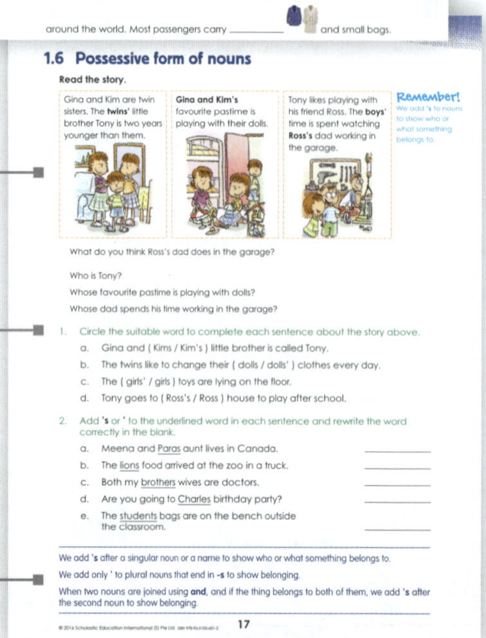

Grammar focus through an engaging picture story

Related exercises for meaningful learning

Simple definition to explain each grammar concept

Practice exercises for meaningful application of the concept

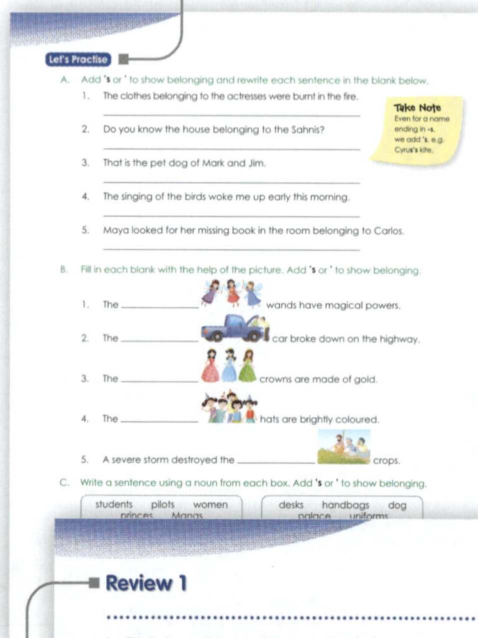

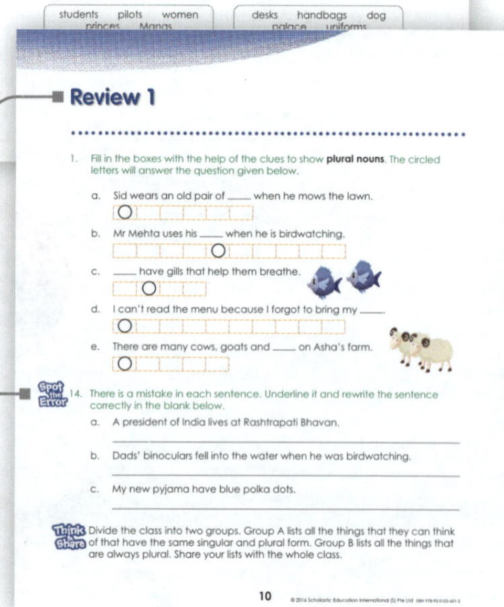

Periodic reviews to consolidate learning and for systematic assessment

Spot the Error to provide an opportunity for error correction

- **Take Note** provides additional tips and exceptions to rules.
- **Think & Share** activities allow opportunity for collaborative learning.
- **Remember** enhances the understanding of the concept being taught in the unit.

 ISBN 978-93-5103-601-2

Graded exercises develop key comprehension and critical thinking skills

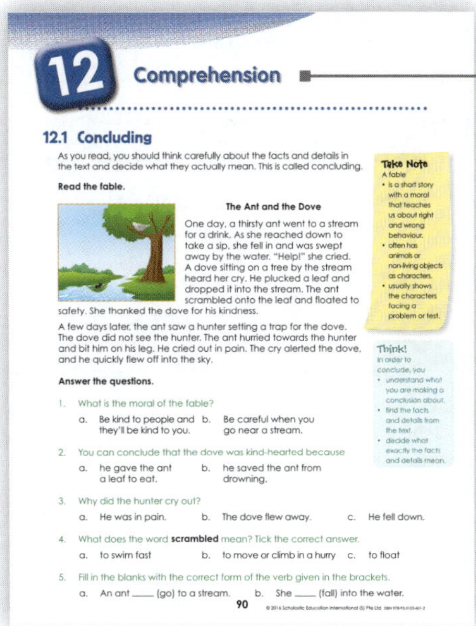

12 Comprehension

12.1 Concluding

As you read, you should think carefully about the facts and details in the text and decide what they actually mean. This is called concluding.

Read the fable.

The Ant and the Dove

One day, a thirsty ant went to a stream for a drink. As she reached down to take a sip, she fell in and was swept away by the water. "Help!" she cried. A dove sitting on a tree by the stream heard her cry. He plucked a leaf and dropped it into the stream. The ant scrambled onto the leaf and floated to safety. She thanked the dove for his kindness.

A few days later, the ant saw a hunter setting a trap for the dove. The dove did not see the hunter. The ant hurried towards the hunter and bit him on his leg. He cried out in pain. The cry alerted the dove, and he quickly flew off into the sky.

Take Note
A fable
- is a short story with a moral that teaches us about right and wrong behaviour.
- often has animals or non-living objects as characters.
- usually shows the characters facing a problem or test.

Think!
In order to conclude, you
- understand what you are making a conclusion about.
- find the facts and details from the text.
- decide what exactly the facts and details mean.

Answer the questions.

1. What is the moral of the fable?
   a. Be kind to people and they'll be kind to you.
   b. Be careful when you go near a stream.
2. You can conclude that the dove was kind-hearted because
   a. he gave the ant a leaf to eat.
   b. he saved the ant from drowning.
3. Why did the hunter cry out?
   a. He was in pain.
   b. The dove flew away.
   c. He fell down.
4. What does the word **scrambled** mean? Tick the correct answer.
   a. to swim fast
   b. to move or climb in a hurry
   c. to float
5. Fill in the blanks with the correct form of the verb given in the brackets.
   a. An ant ___ (go) to a stream.
   b. She ___ (fall) into the water.

90

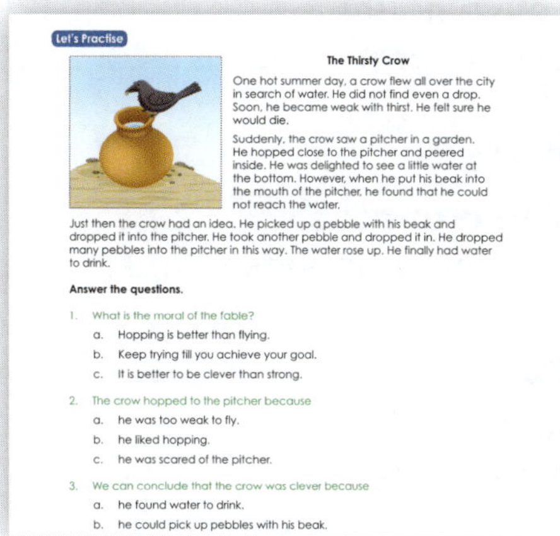

Let's Practise

The Thirsty Crow

One hot summer day, a crow flew all over the city in search of water. He did not find even a drop. Soon, he became weak with thirst. He felt sure he would die.

Suddenly, the crow saw a pitcher in a garden. He hopped close to the pitcher and peered inside. He was delighted to see a little water at the bottom. However, when he put his beak into the mouth of the pitcher, he found that he could not reach the water.

Just then the crow had an idea. He picked up a pebble with his beak and dropped it into the pitcher. He took another pebble and dropped it in. He dropped many pebbles into the pitcher in this way. The water rose up. He finally had water to drink.

Answer the questions.

1. What is the moral of the fable?
   a. Hopping is better than flying.
   b. Keep trying till you achieve your goal.
   c. It is better to be clever than strong.
2. The crow hopped to the pitcher because
   a. he was too weak to fly.
   b. he liked hopping.
   c. he was scared of the pitcher.
3. We can conclude that the crow was clever because
   a. he found water to drink.
   b. he could pick up pebbles with his beak.

Scaffolded exercises to develop key writing skills across varied genres and topics

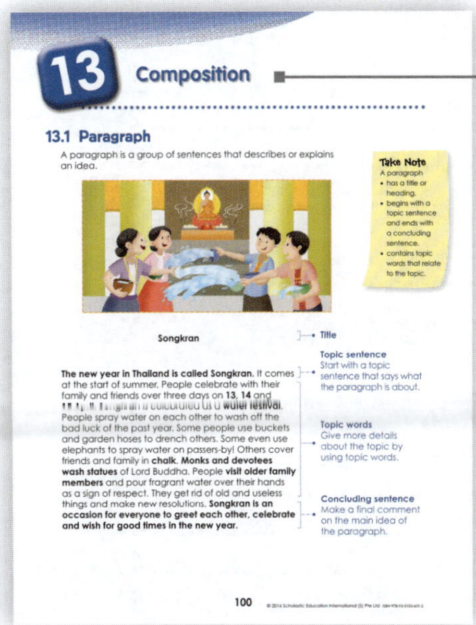

13 Composition

13.1 Paragraph

A paragraph is a group of sentences that describes or explains an idea.

Take Note
A paragraph
- has a title or heading.
- begins with a topic sentence and ends with a concluding sentence.
- contains topic words that relate to the topic.

Songkran — Title

The new year in Thailand is called Songkran. It comes at the start of summer. People celebrate with their family and friends over three days on 13, 14 and 15 April. Songkran is celebrated as a water festival. People spray water on each other to wash off the bad luck of the past year. Some people use buckets and garden hoses to drench others. Some even use elephants to spray water on passers-by! Others cover friends and family in **chalk. Monks and devotees wash statues** of Lord Buddha. People **visit older family members** and pour fragrant water over their hands as a sign of respect. They get rid of old and useless things and make new resolutions. **Songkran is an occasion for everyone to greet each other, celebrate and wish for good times in the new year.**

Topic sentence: Start with a topic sentence that says what the paragraph is about.

Topic words: Give more details about the topic by using topic words.

Concluding sentence: Make a final comment on the main idea of the paragraph.

100

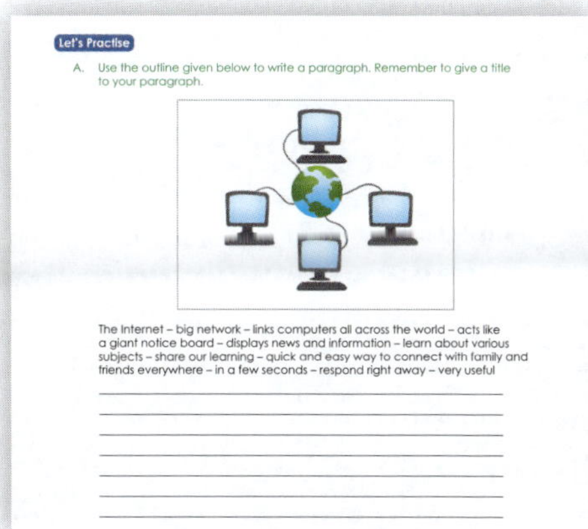

Let's Practise

A. Use the outline given below to write a paragraph. Remember to give a title to your paragraph.

The Internet – big network – links computers all across the world – acts like a giant notice board – displays news and information – learn about various subjects – share our learning – quick and easy way to connect with family and friends everywhere – in a few seconds – respond right away – very useful

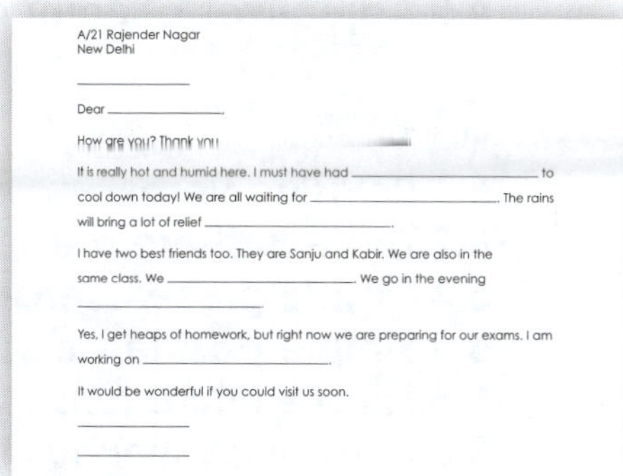

A/21 Rajender Nagar
New Delhi

Dear ___

How are you? Thank you ...

It is really hot and humid here. I must have had ___ to cool down today! We are all waiting for ___. The rains will bring a lot of relief ___.

I have two best friends too. They are Sanju and Kabir. We are also in the same class. We ___. We go in the evening ___.

Yes, I get heaps of homework, but right now we are preparing for our exams. I am working on ___.

It would be wonderful if you could visit us soon.

Vocabulary building through engaging exercises

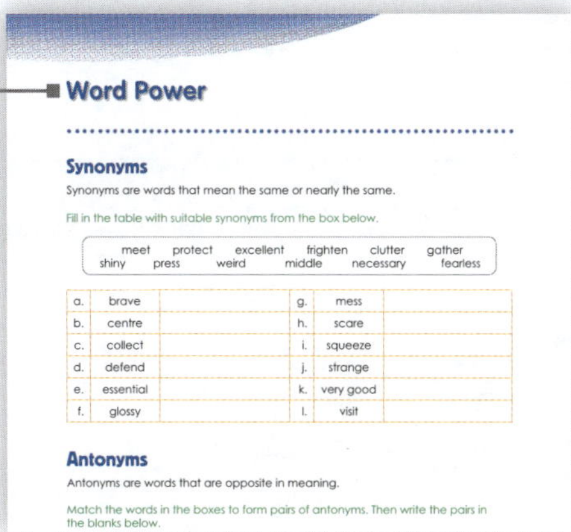

Word Power

Synonyms

Synonyms are words that mean the same or nearly the same.

Fill in the table with suitable synonyms from the box below.

meet protect excellent frighten clutter gather shiny press weird middle necessary fearless

a.	brave		g.	mess	
b.	centre		h.	scare	
c.	collect		i.	squeeze	
d.	defend		j.	strange	
e.	essential		k.	very good	
f.	glossy		l.	visit	

Antonyms

Antonyms are words that are opposite in meaning.

Match the words in the boxes to form pairs of antonyms. Then write the pairs in the blanks below.

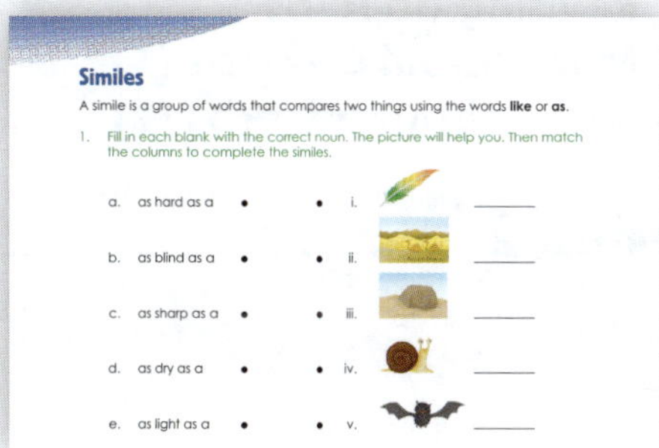

Similes

A simile is a group of words that compares two things using the words **like** or **as**.

1. Fill in each blank with the correct noun. The picture will help you. Then match the columns to complete the similes.

a. as hard as a • • i. ___
b. as blind as a • • ii. ___
c. as sharp as a • • iii. ___
d. as dry as a • • iv. ___
e. as light as a • • v. ___

 ISBN 978-93-5103-601-2

Contents

 ISBN 978-93-5103-601-2

 ISBN 978-93-5103-601-2

1 Nouns

Let's Recall

- Everything around us has a name. These names are called **naming words** or **nouns**.
- Names for people, places, animals and things are called **common nouns**.
- Special names for people, places, animals and things are called **proper nouns**. They always begin with a capital letter.
- Names of days of the week, months and festivals are also proper nouns.
- **He words** such as **boy**, **father** and **tiger** are called **masculine nouns**.
- **She words** such as **girl**, **mother** and **tigress** are called **feminine nouns**.
- Naming words for one person, place, animal or thing are called **singular nouns**.
- Naming words for more than one person, place, animal or thing are called **plural nouns**.
- We make a noun plural by changing or adding letters to the singular noun. For most nouns, we add **-s** to make them plural. For nouns that end in **-s**, **-ss**, **-sh**, **-ch**, **-o** and **-x**, we add **-es**. We replace the **-f** and **-fe** endings of nouns with **-ves** and the **-y** ending with **-ies**.
- The plural form of some nouns is quite different from their singular form.

1.1 Revising nouns

1. Circle the **proper nouns** and underline the **common nouns** in the sentences.

   a. Molly climbed to the top of Mount Everest last year.

   b. Seoul is the capital of South Korea.

   c. Do you know which month comes after April?

   d. We learnt that the Nile is the longest river in the world.

Take Note
Names of rivers, oceans and mountains are also proper nouns.

2. Fill in the blanks with the correct **common nouns**. The pictures will help you.

Our neighbour Palak is friendly and loves travelling. She is a ___________ .

She flies large ___________  loaded with passengers to countries

around the world. Most passengers carry ___________  and small bags.

They collect their ___________  after they land.

 ISBN 978-93-5103-601-2

3. Fill in each blank with the opposite **masculine** or **feminine noun** from the box below.

lady	goose	sister	bridegroom	duke	witch

a. brother ______

b. duchess ______

c. gentleman ______

d. wizard ______

e. bride ______

f. gander ______

4. Fill in each blank with the correct **masculine** or **feminine noun**. The picture will help you.

a. Mary was lost, so she asked a ______  to help her.

b. The ______  ran under a bush and the vixen hid in a hole.

c. Farmer John has a grey ______  and a brown cow.

d. My ______  and aunt live near the mall.

e. The ______  crowed loudly and the ______  clucked in reply.

5. Make sentences using the following pairs of **masculine** and **feminine nouns**.

a. lion – lioness

______

______

b. niece – nephew

______

______

c. ram – ewe

______

______

 ISBN 978-93-5103-601-2

6. Fill in the blanks with the correct **plural** forms of the **nouns** given in the brackets.

a. Lots of ________ (gas) are released when ________ (volcano) erupt.

b. We placed our ________ (scarf) and ________ (key) on the ________ (bench).

c. The doctor's waiting room was full of wailing ________ (baby).

d. In summer, we love picking ________ (mango) from the ________ (tree).

e. Put the ________ (knife) in the ________ (box) and place the ________ (dish) next to the ________ (glass).

Take Note

- The letters **a**, **e**, **i**, **o** and **u** are called **vowels**. All other letters of the alphabet are called **consonants**.
- For nouns that end in a **consonant and y**, we add **-ies**, and for nouns that end in a **vowel and y**, we add **-s** to the singular noun.

7. Fill in each blank with the correct **plural** form of the **noun**.

a. kilo ________

b. hoof ________

c. zoo ________

d. chief ________

e. buffalo ________

Take Note

- For some nouns that end in **-f**, we add only **-s**, e.g. chef – chef**s**. For other nouns ending in **-f**, we either add **-s** or change **-f** to **-ves**, e.g. dwarf – dwarf**s** or dwar**ves**.
- For some nouns that end in **-o**, we add only **-s**, e.g. kangaro**o** – kangaro**os**. For other nouns ending in **-o**, we add either **-s** or **-es**, e.g. mang**o** – mang**os** or mang**oes**.

8. In the grid below, find the **plural** forms of the **nouns** given in the box.

foot goose ox mouse tooth woman child

Z	Q	C	R	G	W	M	S
F	B	M	E	O	Y	S	E
E	O	I	M	O	X	E	N
E	N	C	L	U	T	W	T
T	E	E	T	H	I	O	F
A	O	C	V	S	L	M	T
C	Z	G	E	E	S	E	R
F	E	V	M	Y	T	N	F
R	D	E	N	K	B	P	G
C	H	I	L	D	R	E	N

 ISBN 978-93-5103-601-2

1.2 More about plural nouns

Read the story.

Alice's family went for a hike last weekend. Alice wore her **jeans**. Tom wore his favourite green **shorts**.

There were many **deer** grazing in the field. One **deer** grazed far away near the trees.

Some **sheep** were playing together. One **sheep** stood alone on the hillside.

How does the sheep standing alone feel? Why do you think so?

What did Alice wear for the hike? What did Tom wear?

Which animals grazed in the field?

Which animals were having fun?

1. Fill in each blank with a suitable noun from the story above.

   a. All the ________ at the farm had big antlers.

   b. The woolly coat of a ________ is called fleece.

   c. My favourite ________ got muddy when I lay down by the stream.

2. Rearrange each group of letters to form a plural noun. The picture will help you.

   a. hespe: ________ 

   b. csissosr: ________ 

   c. ssulngases: ________ 

   d. aricarft: ________ 

The **singular** and **plural** forms of some **nouns** are the same, for example, deer, aircraft. Some nouns are always plural, for example, shorts, sunglasses.

 ISBN 978-93-5103-601-2

Let's Practise

A. Fill in each blank with the correct **noun** from the box below.

pyjamas	boots	gloves	trousers	binoculars

1. Mum bought me a pair of leather __________ last week.
2. Amar put on his __________ and climbed into bed.
3. Dad spilt coffee on his new __________.
4. These __________ will help you see things that are far away.
5. If your hands are cold, you should put on a pair of __________.

Take Note

- We usually use **a pair of** with things that have two parts joined together, e.g. scissors, pliers. We also use **a pair of** with some nouns that are made up of a set of two similar things, e.g. **a pair of** boots.
- We use the plural **fishes** when we talk about different kinds of fish.

B. Underline the **plural noun** in each sentence. Then circle it in the word grid below.

1. There were lots of sheep on the farm.
2. Seema used a pair of blue pliers to cut the wire.
3. My grandmother is always losing her spectacles!
4. Nusrat saw a variety of fishes at the aquarium.
5. The doctor told Mum to wear sunglasses when she went out in the sun.

X	C	S	E	R	N	U	I	E	P
D	O	A	F	C	M	K	A	G	A
Q	S	B	V	L	O	U	R	E	F
Y	X	H	P	M	T	E	D	K	I
S	P	E	C	T	A	C	L	E	S
H	J	M	D	E	U	I	L	V	H
E	S	K	P	L	I	E	R	S	E
E	L	Y	F	S	W	T	O	A	S
P	E	P	O	J	I	E	G	H	M
S	U	N	G	L	A	S	S	E	S

Think & Share Divide the class into two groups. Group A lists all the things that they can think of that have the same singular and plural form. Group B lists all the things that are always plural. Share your lists with the whole class.

 ISBN 978-93-5103-601-2

1.3 Common-gender nouns

Read the story.

Atlanta Hotel is very popular with **tourists** visiting our city.

The **receptionist** welcomes all **guests** with a friendly smile.

The restaurant at the hotel serves delicious food. The **cooks** and **chefs** are well trained.

Remember!
Nouns that refer to males are called masculine nouns. Nouns that refer to females are called feminine nouns.

Why do you think Atlanta Hotel is popular?

Who stays at the hotel?

Who welcomes guests to the hotel?

Who works at the hotel's restaurant?

1. Fill in each blank with a suitable noun from the story above.

   a. A ________________ looks at a flyer of the Atlanta Hotel.

   b. The hotel has many rooms for its ________________.

   c. The ________________ works at the main desk.

   d. The ________________ work in the hotel's kitchen.

2. Colour the clouds with nouns that refer to both males and females.

   woman doctor niece

   baby uncle

   principal guest wife

   parent lion

Nouns that are used for both males and females are called **common-gender nouns**.

 ISBN 978-93-5103-601-2

Let's Practise

A. Write **M** for masculine nouns, **F** for feminine nouns and **C** for common-gender nouns. Then make a sentence with each **common-gender noun**.

1.	father	[ ]	7.	friend	[ ]
2.	person	[ ]	8.	student	[ ]
3.	aunt	[ ]	9.	grandmother	[ ]
4.	baker	[ ]	10.	child	[ ]
5.	king	[ ]	11.	woman	[ ]
6.	peahen	[ ]	12.	boar	[ ]

____

____

____

____

____

____

____

____

____

____

____

____

____

B. Write the **nouns** given in the box in the correct column below.

daughter driver prince judge tourist goddess
wizard nephew sister queen thief artist

Feminine nouns	Masculine nouns	Common-gender nouns

 ISBN 978-93-5103-601-2

1.4 Countable and uncountable nouns

Read the story.

Mr Brown has a beautiful **garden**. He uses a **watering can** to water the three new **flowers** that bloomed this **morning**.

Suddenly, the **rain** comes down. Mr Brown goes inside. He stands at a **window** and drinks his **coffee**.

Coco rushes in. He spatters **water** all over and brings **mud** into the **house**!

Do you think Mrs Brown is upset? What do you think she will say to Coco?

How many new flowers are there in the garden?

How many watering cans can you see in the garden?

What does Coco do after getting wet in the rain?

1. Fill in each blank with a suitable noun from the story above.
   a. How many ________ are there in the vase?
   b. Coco likes getting wet in the ________.
   c. Mrs Brown was upset with Coco for bringing ________ into the house.
   d. Mr and Mrs Brown have a lovely ________.

2. Complete the table with nouns from the story.

Nouns for things we can count	**Nouns for things we cannot count**
Example flowers	mud

Nouns for things we can count are called **countable nouns**, for example, garden. Nouns for things we cannot count are called **uncountable nouns**, for example, rain.

 ISBN 978-93-5103-601-2

Let's Practise

A. Colour the **countable nouns** red and the **uncountable nouns** green in the table below.

cheese	phone	tea	sand
tree	snow	snake	rice
bottle	salt	flag	park
wood	umbrella	sugar	wool
playground	water	juice	dog
train	sister	air	milk

B. Fill in each blank with **a**, **an** or **some** and a suitable **noun**. The picture will help you.

1. There is ________  in the cup.
2. I saw ________  in the park.
3. Have ________  before you sleep.

4. Here is ________  for you to draw on.
5. The children were excited to see ________  at the zoo.
6. Venky packed ________  and crackers for the picnic.

Take Note

- Countable nouns have a singular and a plural form. We usually use **a** or **an** with the singular form, e.g. **a** flower, and words such as **many** and **a few** with the plural form, e.g. **many** flowers.
- We use words such as **some**, **much**, **a little** and **a lot of** with uncountable nouns, e.g. **some** grass.

Think & Share Pair up with a classmate and play a "Counting Nouns" game. Think of a countable noun and ask your partner to suggest an uncountable noun that goes with it, for example, bottle – milk. Make a list of the countable and uncountable nouns you come up with. Share your list with the class.

 ISBN 978-93-5103-601-2

1.5 Collective nouns

Read the story.

The Kumar **family** are having a barbecue in their garden. The children help to set the table.

Soni places a **bunch** of red flowers from the garden in a vase on the table.

Oh no! A **swarm** of bees is heading their way. That's the end of their barbecue!

Does the family look excited in the first picture? How do you think they feel in the last picture? Why?

Who is having a barbecue?

What does Soni place in the vase?

Why does the family look upset?

1. Read the sentences in the pictures above. Match the words that go together.

a.	bees •	• i.	family
b.	flowers •	• ii.	swarm
c.	people •	• iii.	bunch

2. Rearrange each group of letters to form a noun. The picture will help you.

a. a (bndule) ________ of sticks 

b. a (hbucn) ________ of keys 

c. a (cshloo) ________ of fish 

d. a (hrde) ________ of elephants 

Words for groups of people, animals and things are called **collective nouns**.

 ISBN 978-93-5103-601-2

Let's Practise

A. Fill in each blank with the correct **collective noun** from the box.

bundle	flock	team	class	pack

1. Our ________ will go on a field trip this Thursday.
2. Divya tied the ________ of sticks together.
3. A ________ of wolves lives in that cave.
4. Can you see that ________ of birds in the sky?
5. The ________ will play a match in Delhi tomorrow.

B. Underline the **collective nouns** in the sentences.

1. Tania bought a new pack of cards for the train journey.
2. A flock of sheep grazes in the field.
3. This chest of drawers will be perfect for our room.
4. We spotted a swarm of butterflies near the lake.
5. A gang of thieves attacked the store.
6. Look at that litter of puppies!
7. The herd of giraffes was chased by a pride of lions.
8. The crowd cheered when Dan scored a goal.

C. Circle the correct **collective noun** to complete each sentence.

1. Rahul and his (band / pack) of musicians have a concert on Saturday.
2. There is a (litter / pile) of books on the table.
3. I bought a (crew / bouquet) of flowers for my best friend.
4. Alka gave her mother a (string / bunch) of pearls on her birthday.
5. Please place this (stack / bundle) of chairs beside that table.

D. Tick the correct box for each **noun** given below.

1.	corn	sheaf	☐	sheet	☐
2.	bananas	team	☐	bunch	☐
3.	stairs	crew	☐	flight	☐
4.	soldiers	army	☐	flock	☐
5.	children	troop	☐	pile	☐

Take Note

- Collective nouns are usually singular, but can sometimes have a plural doing word, e.g. The **crew** of sailors **is/are** resting.
- Most collective nouns refer to groups of the same kind, e.g. an **army** of soldiers.
- Some collective nouns can be used for groups of different kinds, e.g. a **herd** of cattle, **luggage**.
- Some collective nouns may be used on their own without mentioning the people, animals or things they refer to, e.g. **team**.

 ISBN 978-93-5103-601-2

1.6 Possessive form of nouns

Read the story.

Gina and Kim are twin sisters. The **twins'** little brother Tony is two years younger than them.

Gina and Kim's favourite pastime is playing with their dolls.

Tony likes playing with his friend Ross. The **boys'** time is spent watching **Ross's** dad working in the garage.

Remember!
We add **'s** to nouns to show who or what something belongs to.

What do you think Ross's dad does in the garage?

Who is Tony?

Whose favourite pastime is playing with dolls?

Whose dad spends his time working in the garage?

1. Circle the suitable word to complete each sentence about the story above.

   a. Gina and (Kims / Kim's) little brother is called Tony.

   b. The twins like to change their (dolls / dolls') clothes every day.

   c. The (girls' / girls) toys are lying on the floor.

   d. Tony goes to (Ross's / Ross) house to play after school.

2. Add **'s** or **'** to the underlined word in each sentence and rewrite the word correctly in the blank.

   a. Meena and <u>Paras</u> aunt lives in Canada. __________

   b. The <u>lions</u> food arrived at the zoo in a truck. __________

   c. Both my <u>brothers</u> wives are doctors. __________

   d. Are you going to <u>Charles</u> birthday party? __________

   e. The <u>students</u> bags are on the bench outside the classroom. __________

We add **'s** after a singular noun or a name to show who or what something belongs to.

We add only **'** to plural nouns that end in **-s** to show belonging.

When two nouns are joined using **and**, and if the thing belongs to both of them, we add **'s** after the second noun to show belonging.

 ISBN 978-93-5103-601-2

Let's Practise

A. Add **'s** or **'** to show belonging and rewrite each sentence in the blank below.

1. The clothes belonging to the actresses were burnt in the fire.

   ____

2. Do you know the house belonging to the Sahnis?

   ____

3. That is the pet dog of Mark and Jim.

   ____

4. The singing of the birds woke me up early this morning.

   ____

5. Maya looked for her missing book in the room belonging to Carlos.

   ____

Take Note
Even for a name ending in **-s**, we add **'s**, e.g. Cyrus**'s** kite.

B. Fill in each blank with the help of the picture. Add **'s** or **'** to show belonging.

1. The ______________  wands have magical powers.
2. The ______________  car broke down on the highway.
3. The ______________  crowns are made of gold.
4. The ______________  hats are brightly coloured.
5. A severe storm destroyed the ______________  crops.

C. Write a sentence using a noun from each box. Add **'s** or **'** to show belonging.

students pilots women princes Manas	desks handbags dog palace uniforms

1. ____________________
2. ____________________
3. ____________________
4. ____________________
5. ____________________

 ISBN 978-93-5103-601-2

2 Pronouns

Let's Recall

- Naming words are called **nouns**.
- The words **I**, **we**, **you**, **he**, **she**, **it** and **they** and **me**, **us**, **you**, **him**, **her**, **it** and **them** can take the place of nouns. These words are called **pronouns**.

2.1 Revising pronouns

1. Fill in each blank with a **pronoun**. The picture will help you.

   a. Aditi has an extra sweet. Do you want ________?

   b. Hello! Our names are Anu, Divi and Rani. ________ are cousins.

   c. Kapil likes taking pictures. So ________ bought a camera.

   d. Elephants live in herds. ________ take care of one another.

2. Read the story carefully. Then circle the **pronouns**.

Take Note
The pronoun **it** can be used for babies, animals and things.

Niti and Ramesh wanted to do something special for Mum on Mother's Day.

"We can make breakfast for her!" said Niti. Their little brother, Dhruv, wanted to help them. So they told him to toast bread in the toaster while they made some eggs and tea. He toasted a slice of bread and spread butter and jam on it.

Mum entered the kitchen. She said, "How kind! Have you two made breakfast for me?"

Dhruv piped in to say, "I helped, too!"

"Yes, Mum, all three of us made your breakfast together," said Ramesh.

 ISBN 978-93-5103-601-2

2.2 More about pronouns

Read the story.

Do you think Reena likes Suhani's suggestions? Why do you think so?

Which words does Suhani use when she refers to herself?

Which word does Reena use when she refers to Suhani?

Which words does Suhani use when she refers to Reena and herself?

1. Fill in the blanks with pronouns from the story above.

   a. "________ have an idea, Ruth!" said Freddie. "Why don't ________ bake a cake for Mum?"

   b. "________ must visit ________ soon," said Mr and Mrs Rao to their neighbour.

   c. "Can ________ give ________ an idea when the dress will be ready?" Padma asked the tailor.

2. Fill in each blank with the correct pronoun from the box below.

me	I	you	we	us

   a. My name is Nina. ________ am an engineer.

   b. My brother and I enjoy painting. ________ often paint together.

   c. Lina, ________ need to submit this form by tomorrow.

   d. Our friends are important to ________.

   e. Here is a picture of ________ when I was in kindergarten.

The pronouns **I**, **me**, **we** and **us** take the place of the person or people speaking. The pronoun **you** takes the place of the person or people being spoken to.

 ISBN 978-93-5103-601-2

Let's Practise

A. Fill in each blank with the correct **pronoun**. The picture will help you.

Remember!

- **I** and **me** are used when referring to one person.
- **We** and **us** are used when referring to two or more people.
- **You** is used when referring to one or more than one person.

1. Mohan helped ________  to climb up the apple tree.

2. My name is Vinny. ________  wear glasses and have brown hair.

3. Sally and I are going to the summer camp. ________  like camping.

4. Our Maths teacher has asked ________  to study for a test next week.

5. Would ________  like to come with me to the market?

B. Circle the correct **pronoun** to complete each sentence.

1. Mum, may I go trekking with ____?
   a. we b. you c. us
2. Can you tell ____ the way to the bus stop?
   a. I b. me c. you
3. ____ are going to Disneyland for a holiday next year.
   a. Us b. I c. We
4. Our elder brother picks ____ up from school on Fridays.
   a. us b. we c. I
5. ____ have a cousin who lives in Canada.
   a. Us b. I c. Me

Think & Share Pair up with a classmate to play the game "A day in my life". Take turns to speak about yourself and a day in your life using as many pronouns as you can. Your partner keeps count of the number of pronouns you use. Compare your pronoun scores once you have both had a turn.

 ISBN 978-93-5103-601-2

3 Articles

Let's Recall

- We use the words **a**, **an** and **the** before nouns. They are called **articles**.
- We use **a** when the first letter of the noun is a consonant.
- We use **an** when the first letter of the noun is a vowel or when a noun starts with a vowel sound.
- We use **the** for a particular thing and with nouns that are one of a kind.

3.1 Revising articles

1. Fill in each blank with **a**, **an** or **the**. The picture will help you.

   a. Please bring ________  along for the picnic tomorrow.

   b. I cannot find my keys anywhere in ________ .

   c. Sonia uses ________  to draw pictures in her sketchbook.

   d. ________  with a green cap is my brother.

   e. ________  has craters in its surface.

   f. Akbar baked two cakes. ________  were delicious.

Remember!
We use **the** before a noun
- to refer to a subject mentioned earlier, e.g. Rita bought a book. **The** book was very interesting.
- when it is clear which person or thing we are talking about, e.g. My cousin lives in **the** house across **the** park.

2. Make a sentence using the jumbled words given below. Add **a**, **an** or **the** before each noun.

   a. lives beehive in bee

   ____

   b. writing am I e-mail to principal

   ____

   c. time now what is

   ____

   d. is training become she astronaut to

   ____

Remember!
A sentence begins with a capital letter and ends with a full stop or question mark.

 ISBN 978-93-5103-601-2

3.2 More uses of *the*

Read the story.

The Eiffel Tower is a famous monument in Paris.

It can be seen from across **the** River Seine. Many tourists visit France each year to see it.

The French are famous for their fashionable clothes. Tourists enjoy shopping in the streets of Paris.

Does your city have any famous monument? What is its name?

Which is the most famous monument in Paris?

Which river runs through Paris?

Who are famous for being fashionable?

1. Note the sentences in the story above. Now add the missing article in the correct place in each sentence below.
   a. Have you visited Eiffel Tower?
   b. There are many bridges over River Seine.
   c. French are proud of their monuments.

2. Underline the correct uses of **the** and circle the incorrect uses of **the** in the sentences below.
   a. The Colosseum in the Rome is very popular with tourists.
   b. The Ganges is the holy river of the Hindus.
   c. The Pacific Ocean is the largest ocean in the world.
   d. The Japanese enjoy eating the seafood.
   e. The Statue of Liberty is a famous monument in the New York.

We use the article **the** before the names of important buildings, rivers and oceans. We also use **the** before the names of important books and mountains.

We use the article **the** with some nationality words, for example, **the** French/Chinese, to mean the French/Chinese people.

 ISBN 978-93-5103-601-2

Let's Practise

A. Read the passage carefully. Rewrite it in your notebook, adding the article **the** where needed and crossing it out where it is used incorrectly.

Taj Mahal is the most famous monument of the India. It is in the Agra, a city in northern India. It is the situated along River Yamuna. Taj Mahal was built more than the 400 years ago by the Shah Jahan, Mughal emperor. He built Taj Mahal in memory of his beloved wife. Thousands of people worked together to build Taj Mahal. Tourists from the all over world come to see this beautiful monument in white marble.

B. Make sentences using each group of words below. Remember to use the article **the** where needed.

Example koala sleep nearly 18 hours day

The koala can sleep for nearly 18 hours a day.

1. Dinosaur prehistoric animal

____

2. Mount Everest in Himalayas

____

3. Sahara Desert very little rain

____

4. Dutch prefer cycling driving

____

Take Note

- When we talk about plural nouns in general, we don't use any article. For example, **Dinosaurs** are prehistoric animals. **Malaysians** like spicy food.
- We use **the** before a singular noun that stands for a whole class, for example, **the lion**.

Think & Share Pair up with a classmate. Choose a story or a newspaper article. Read out the story to your partner without the three articles – **a**, **an** and **the**. Ask your partner if they were able to understand the story. Discuss why articles are important.

 ISBN 978-93-5103-601-2

Review 1

1. Fill in the boxes with the help of the clues to show **plural nouns**. The circled letters will answer the question given below.

   a. Sid wears an old pair of ____ when he mows the lawn.

   b. Mr Mehta uses his ____ when he is birdwatching.

   c. ____ have gills that help them breathe.

   d. I can't read the menu because I forgot to bring my ____.

   e. There are many cows, goats and ____ on Asha's farm.

   f. Farooq wore a white shirt and black ____ to the interview.

   g. ____ grow new antlers each year.

   h. My brother says the patch on his favourite pair of ____ looks cool.

   What do you use to cut paper? ______________

2. Circle the incorrect **plural nouns** in the box below. Then write the correct forms in the blanks and use them in sentences of your own.

aircrafts	reindeer	pyjama	sunglasses
goggle	goldfish	tong	

   a. ______________________________

   b. ______________________________

   c. ______________________________

   d. ______________________________

 ISBN 978-93-5103-601-2

3. Complete the table below by writing the names of people you know next to each **common-gender noun**.

	Common-gender noun	Female	Male
a.	baby		
b.	child		
c.	doctor		
d.	friend		

4. Underline the **common-gender nouns** in the story given below.

The manager of Kookie's Coffee Shop was very happy. There were many people in the coffee shop that day. They were all hockey fans, and had gathered there to celebrate the victory of their team. It was an important celebration. Even the players and their captain joined them.

5. Fill in each blank with a **countable noun** that can be used with the **uncountable noun** below.

Example water bottle

a. coffee ________

b. tea ________

c. milk ________

d. juice ________

6. Tick the sentences where the **uncountable nouns** are used correctly.

a. There was a lot of grass covering the field. ☐

b. Please give me fifteen paper. ☐

c. The mat had some sand on it. ☐

d. We had many snow last year. ☐

e. The rain washed away many soil. ☐

7. Unscramble the letters to form a **collective noun**.

a. a ________ (rehd) of buffaloes

b. a ________ (casls) of students

c. a ________ (maet) of players

d. a ________ (abnd) of thieves

e. a ________ (trelit) of cubs

f. a ________ (wdcro) of spectators

 ISBN 978-93-5103-601-2

8. Circle the correct **collective noun** in each sentence.

a. An angry (swarm / family) of bees flew out of the bushes.

b. The (flock / fleet) of ships set sail at the crack of dawn.

c. We had to climb a steep (flight / flock) of stairs to get here.

d. Mum looked everywhere for her (bunch / pack) of keys.

e. A (swarm / flock) of birds gathered on the terrace.

9. Rewrite the sentences in your notebook, adding **'s** or **'** in the correct place.

a. I think Rohans science project is very informative.

b. Mrs Das house is across the road from the city library.

c. The butterflies wings looked transparent in the sunlight.

d. The five girls performance was appreciated by the audience.

e. Leyla and Abbas flight is scheduled to arrive at 10 p.m.

10. Tick the correct word(s) to complete each sentence.

a. A ________ baby is called a pup.

i. bat's ii. bats's iii. bats

b. All the ________ sports equipment is in the basement.

i. students' ii. student's iii. student

c. The ________ coats were hanging in the cupboard.

i. ladies ii. ladies' iii. ladies's

d. My friend ________ family comes from Switzerland.

i. Thomas' ii. Thomas's iii. Thoma's

e. This ________ front seat is too small for me.

i. cars's ii. car's iii. cars

f. ________ sister is ten years old.

i. Tim and Dan's ii. Tim's and Dan iii. Tim's and Dan's

11. Circle the **pronouns** in the story.

Last week, Mrs Morris told us about earthquakes. I asked if earthquakes could be predicted before they happened. Mrs Morris said, "Can you think of a way to find out the answer?" At lunchtime, I looked for books about earthquakes at the library. My friend Jim helped me with my research. We borrowed four books and decided to read two each. After a week, we had the answer. We will share it with Mrs Morris tomorrow.

 ISBN 978-93-5103-601-2

12. Fill in each blank with the correct **pronoun** from the brackets.

a. The security guard told ________ that the gates would open at 9 a.m. (me/I)

b. ________ am typing an e-mail on Mum's computer. (Me/I)

c. The tour guide took ________ inside the old fort. (us/I)

d. Our bus arrived twenty minutes after ________ reached the bus stop. (we/me)

e. ________ can all play with my toys. (You/I)

13. Rewrite each sentence using the article **the** where needed.

a. Great Wall of China is one of wonders of world.

____

b. River Nile flows through Egypt.

____

c. Volunteers are working to keep Yamuna clean.

____

d. Orca is also known as killer whale.

____

e. India is surrounded by Arabian Sea, Indian Ocean and Bay of Bengal.

____

Spot the Error

14. There is a mistake in each sentence. Underline it and rewrite the sentence correctly in the blank below.

a. A president of India lives at Rashtrapati Bhavan.

____

b. Dads' binoculars fell into the water when he was birdwatching.

____

c. My new pyjama have blue polka dots.

____

d. Aunt Mary asked for much sugar with her coffee.

____

e. My cat's team of kittens follows her all around the house.

____

f. The mosquitoes buzzing annoyed me all through the night.

____

g. The principal called I to her office after assembly.

____

h. A pineapple is a fruit grown in warm countries.

____

 ISBN 978-93-5103-601-2

4 Adjectives

Let's Recall

- **Describing words** tell us more about nouns. A describing word is called an **adjective**.
- Adjectives can describe the shape, size and colour of a noun.
- An adjective is often placed before the noun it is describing, for example, I see a **large** spider on the wall.
- An adjective can also be placed after the noun it describes, that is, after the doing words **is/was** and **are/were**, for example, The coffee is **hot**.
- A **number** can be an adjective. It tells how many people, places, animals or things there are, for example, **seven** days.
- When we **compare** two nouns, we often add **-r** or **-er** to the adjective or replace the **-y** ending with **-ier** to form adjectives of comparison, for example, close – **closer**, slow – **slower**, noisy – **noisier**.
- We add the word **more** before longer adjectives instead of changing their ending. We also often use the word **than** after adjectives of comparison, for example, This sofa is **more comfortable than** that chair.
- We use the adjectives **my**, **our**, **your**, **his**, **her**, **its** and **their** with a noun to show that it belongs to someone or something.

4.1 Revising adjectives

1. Fill in each blank with a suitable **adjective**. The picture will help you.

   a. Aisha is wearing ________ socks. 

   b. He has a ________ eraser. 

   c. ________ balloons floated in the sky. 

   d. Leave your ________ shoes outside. 

   e. They were ________ because they won the first prize. 

   f. The day was ________ so we wore hats. 

 ISBN 978-93-5103-601-2

2. Fill in each blank with a **number**. The picture will help you.

Remember!
Numbers are used only with countable nouns.

a. Tina gave me ________ beads. 

b. My brother got ________ new T-shirts for his birthday! 

c. ________ students are going in for the quiz competition today. 

d. There are ________ ladybirds on the leaf. 

e. Dad bought ________ cucumbers at the market. 

3. Form an **adjective of comparison** from the adjective given in the brackets, and write it in the blank.

a. I am ________________ than my sister. (tall)
b. Bina is ________________ than her brother. (playful)
c. Who is ________________ than Ken? (charming)
d. This round stone is ________________ than the flat one. (heavy)
e. My dog is ________________ than your cat. (small)
f. Which of these two pieces of string is ________________? (long)
g. Rohan is ________________ than Rakesh. (strong)
h. This chair is ________________ than that one. (comfortable)

4. Tick the correct **adjective** to complete each sentence below.

Take Note
The word **it's** is not an adjective. It is a short form of the words **it is**.

a. The dog was very hungry, so it ate all ____ food quickly.
   i. their   ii. it's   iii. its
b. ____ painting is displayed outside the classroom.
   i. My   ii. Its   iii. It's
c. This parcel belongs to you. It has ____ name on it.
   i. my   ii. your   iii. his
d. This is not my mother's mug. The green one is ____ mug.
   i. his   ii. her   iii. its
e. ____ apartment is small, but it is very comfortable.
   i. Our   ii. Its   iii. It's

 ISBN 978-93-5103-601-2

4.2 Kinds of adjectives

Read the story.

Mr Lee has an **old** mango tree in his backyard. Every year, he picks **raw** mangoes in the **hot** summer.

He peels away the **smooth** skin of the mangoes with a **steel** knife.

With **quick** movements, he mashes the **chopped** mangoes in a **wooden** bowl.

What do you think Mr Lee plans to make with the mangoes?

Which word describes the mango tree?

Which word describes the mango skin?

What kind of bowl does Mr Lee use?

1. Read the story again. Circle the right adjective in the brackets to replace the underlined word.

   a. Mangoes become ripe in the <u>cold</u> season. (old / hot)

   b. Mr Lee picks the mangoes from the tree with <u>slow</u> movements. (sharp / quick)

   c. He puts the <u>sliced</u> mangoes in a bowl. (chopped / smooth)

2. Fill in each blank with words from the box below.

pretty	smooth	young	ancient	quick	old	slow
hot	rough	steel	icy	wooden	shiny	plastic

   a. Describes what something is made of: ______________________

   b. Describes how something/someone looks: ______________________

   c. Describes how old or young something/someone is: ______________________

   d. Describes how fast or slow something/someone is: ______________________

   e. Describes how hot or cold something/someone is: ______________________

   f. Describes what something/someone is or feels like: ______________________

Adjectives are of different kinds. They can describe the material, appearance, age, speed, temperature or quality of nouns.

 ISBN 978-93-5103-601-2

Let's Practise

A. Fill in the blanks in the story with **adjectives** of material, appearance, age, temperature or quality. The picture will help you.

One day an ________ donkey was walking through a meadow. It was a ________ day, and the donkey was ________. There was a ________ stream flowing nearby. Someone had left a ________ bucket filled with water near the stream. The donkey drank from the bucket. He walked for a while, then stopped to smell the ________ flowers and admire the ________ butterflies. Soon, he fell asleep under a ________ tree and only woke up in the evening. It was a wonderful day!

B. Use **adjectives** of material, appearance, age, speed, temperature or quality to describe each noun given below.

1. Your house

____

____

2. Your classroom

____

____

3. Your school bus

____

____

Think & Share Divide the class into two groups. One group lists all the nouns in the classroom and shares the list with the class. The other group thinks of different kinds of adjectives to describe each noun. Combine the two to make a class list.

 ISBN 978-93-5103-601-2

4.3 More about adjectives

Read the story.

Every month, Joy spends **a little** time at the shops. Today, she visits a shop to look at **some** scarves.

Next, she stops at a jewellery shop. She likes **many** necklaces in the display case.

Joy does not want to spend too **much** money. She buys two necklaces at the shop.

Do you think Joy likes shopping? Why do you think so?

How much time does Joy spend at the shops?

How many necklaces does Joy like?

Why does Joy buy only two necklaces?

1. Replace the underlined groups of words with an adjective from the story above.
   a. Joy has a small amount of money that she wants to spend.
   b. She visits a shop to look at a number of scarves.
   c. She admires a large number of necklaces in the display case.
   d. She does not want to spend a lot of money on the necklaces.

2. Underline the adjective in each sentence given below.
   a. May I have some soup?
   b. Please add a little salt to the lemonade.
   c. Andy does not have much work to do.
   d. We went to Goa for a holiday many years ago.
   e. Miriam spent a little time with me today.
   f. Pia saw some crows sitting on the gate.

We use **adjectives** such as **many**, **much**, **some** and **a little** to describe the amount or quantity of something without giving the exact number or amount.

 ISBN 978-93-5103-601-2

Let's Practise

A. Circle the correct **adjective** to complete each sentence.

1. Please try (much / a little) biryani. I think you'll like it.
2. Mum doesn't like too (many / much) sugar in her tea.
3. How (many / some) colours can you see in a rainbow?
4. The beekeeper took (much / some) honey out of the beehive.
5. There wasn't (much / some) time left for a game after lunch.
6. There weren't (a little / many) tourists at India Gate on Monday.

B. Fill in each blank with an **adjective**. The picture will help you.

1.  ________ rain
2.  ________ dewdrops
3.  ________ buildings
4. 

________ toothpaste

C. Make a sentence using each group of words.

1. many cars

____

2. some juice

____

3. a little paint

____

4. much snow

____

Take Note

- We usually use **many** with countable nouns.
- We usually use **a little** and **much** with uncountable nouns.
- We use **some** with both countable and uncountable nouns.
- When we use **many** and **much** with **was not** or **were not**, we often use the short forms of the verbs, e.g. There **wasn't much** money to buy a present. There **weren't many** apples left on the tree.

 ISBN 978-93-5103-601-2

4.4 This, that, these, those

Read the story.

Jamie helps Mr Alva in his workshop. "What are **those** tools for?" he asks.

"I need **that** saw to cut **this** plank of wood," says Mr Alva. "Be careful, it's very sharp."

"Wow! So you made all **these** beautiful things with **those** tools!" says Jamie.

What kind of things does Mr Alva make in his workshop?

What does Jamie ask Mr Alva?

What does Mr Alva reply?

Why is Jamie impressed?

1. Read the story again. Circle the adjective that belongs to the underlined noun in each sentence below.

   a. There are many useful tools in this <u>workshop</u>.

   b. You can use that <u>saw</u> to cut through wood.

   c. Mr Alva made these <u>things</u> in his workshop.

   d. Those <u>tools</u> on the wall are used to make things from wood.

2. Match the picture with the sentence.

a.		i.	I live in that house.
b.		ii.	Those boxes are red.
c.		iii.	My sister bought this watch.
d.		iv.	These shoes are new.

We use **this**, **that**, **these** and **those** before nouns to show which noun we mean. We use **this** for singular nouns which are near and **that** for singular nouns which are far away. We use **these** for plural nouns which are near and **those** for plural nouns which are far away.

 ISBN 978-93-5103-601-2

Let's Practise

A. Tick the sentences where **this**, **that**, **these** and **those** are used as **adjectives**.

1. I love school. These are the best days of my life. ☐
2. That horse is limping because it has a sore leg. ☐
3. This wallet belongs to someone on that street. ☐
4. I will ask Anna if she can mend these jeans. ☐
5. This is my favourite place to read in peace. ☐
6. Those houses on the hill get the best view of the city. ☐
7. That is the book I gave you last year. ☐
8. Adam bought ten boxes of those magnets. ☐

Remember!
When **this**, **that**, **these** and **those** are placed before nouns, they act as adjectives, e.g. **This** kitten belongs to me. When they replace the noun in a sentence, they act as pronouns, e.g. **This** is my kitten.

B. Fill in the blanks with **this**, **that**, **these** and **those**.

Dad came to my room ________ evening. He saw ________ books piled in the corner and ________ dirty plate on my table. "Your room looks very untidy ________ days," he said. I immediately rushed around tidying my room.

C. Match the two columns to make a complete sentence.

1.	Do you see those	•	• a.	cherries are ready to eat?
2.	I'm writing in this	•	• b.	hot-air balloons in the sky?
3.	Do you think these	•	• c.	hook on the wall.
4.	Please hang your bag on that	•	• d.	notebook about my zoo adventure.

D. Circle the correct word to complete each sentence.

1. (Those / That) cats are very friendly.
2. Maxim made (these / this) dish for the first time today.
3. Mr Arya bought (that / these) shoes for his daughter.
4. If I stretch a little I can reach (those / that) shelf.
5. The paint on (that / those) door took a long time to dry.

Think & Share Pair up with a classmate. Take turns to point at different object(s) in the classroom and make a sentence which uses the object(s) and **this**, **that**, **these** or **those**.

 ISBN 978-93-5103-601-2

4.5 Adjectives of comparison

Read the story.

Tom and Lei practise a lot. They are the **most talented** violin-players in Beijing.

December is the **busiest** month for them. They are invited to play at many concerts!

They are the **youngest** musicians to perform at the **most famous** theatre in China.

Remember!

- To compare two nouns, we add **-r**, **-er** or **more** to the adjective, e.g. young – **younger**, beautiful – **more beautiful**.
- For some adjectives, the last letter is doubled before adding the **-er**, e.g. hot + t + er = **hotter**.

Do you think it is important to practise to be good at something? Why?

Which adjectives describe Tom and Lei?

Which adjective describes December?

Which special place did Tom and Lei perform at?

1. From the story above, match the adjective with the noun it describes.

a.	most talented •	• i.	musicians
b.	busiest •	• ii.	violin-players
c.	youngest •	• iii.	theatre
d.	most famous •	• iv.	month

2. Underline the adjectives that compare nouns in the sentences below.

   a. Harsh is the strongest of all his brothers.
   b. The giraffe is the tallest animal on Earth.
   c. This is the most exciting news I have heard all day!
   d. I find Maths the easiest subject of all.
   e. Suman's dog is the most playful dog in the neighbourhood.
   f. Damon is the most careful driver among us.

To **compare** three or more nouns, we add **-est** to the adjective, for example, young – youngest. We add the word **most** before longer adjectives, instead of changing their ending, for example, beautiful – most beautiful.

 ISBN 978-93-5103-601-2

Let's Practise

A. Fill in each blank with the correct **adjective of comparison**. The adjective given in the brackets will help you.

1. This is the ______________ room in the house. (long)
2. George Street is the ______________ street in the city. (busy)
3. Sue knows the ______________ way to the lake. (quick)
4. Henry is the ______________ boy we know. (handsome)
5. Madan has the ______________ pillow in the dormitory. (soft)
6. These flowers have the ______________ smell. (pleasant)
7. Shipra is the ______________ person I have ever met. (thoughtful)
8. Our trip to Italy was the ______________ vacation of my life. (exciting)

B. Look at the pictures below. Make a sentence for each using the **-est** or **most** form of comparison of the **adjective** given.

1.  expensive ______________________________

2.  young ______________________________

3.  tall ______________________________

4.  fast ______________________________

5. 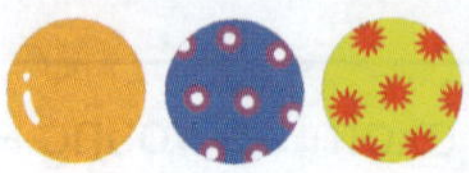 colourful ______________________________

Take Note

- When we use the **-est** form of the adjective, we usually use the word **the** before it, e.g. Dad is **the oldest** member in our family.
- We also add **the** before an adjective that compares nouns using the word **most**, e.g. Ria is **the most intelligent** girl I know.
- For adjectives ending in **-e**, we add **-st**, e.g. large – **largest**.
- For adjectives that end in a consonant and have a vowel before the consonant, we double the consonant and then add **-est** to the adjective, e.g. big – **biggest**.
- For adjectives ending in **-y**, we change the **y** to **i**, and then add **-est** to the adjective, e.g. dirty – **dirtiest**.

 ISBN 978-93-5103-601-2

5 Verbs

Let's Recall

- Words that tell us about an action are called **doing words**. A doing word is called a **verb**.
- The verbs **is**, **am** and **are** are different ways of saying **be**. They introduce a fact about a person, place, animal or thing. They are known as **main verbs** when they are the only verbs in a sentence, for example, She **is** a student.
- When we use the verbs **is**, **am** and **are** with other verbs ending in **-ing**, they are called **helping verbs**, for example, He **is eating** an apple.
- We use the verbs **was** and **were** when we talk about something that happened in the past.
- We use **was** with singular nouns and the pronouns **I**, **it**, **he** and **she**.
- We use **were** with plural nouns and the pronouns **you**, **we** and **they**.
- We use the verbs **has** and **have** to show that something belongs to someone or some other thing.
- We use the verb **had** to show that something belonged to someone or some other thing in the past. We also use it to talk about something that has already happened or about things that affected us. We also use **had** to say what we ate or drank, for example, He **had** a coffee at the snack bar.
- The form of the verb that tells us when an action takes place is called its **tense**. We use the **simple present tense** for actions as they happen. We add **-d** or **-ed** to the verb for actions that happened in the past. This is called the **simple past tense**.

5.1 Revising verbs

1. Replace the incorrect underlined **verb** with the correct one. The picture will help you.

a. Dia runs to her neighbour. 

b. The postman writes on the door. 

c. Aman and his father drive the car. 

d. Joe and Rehan kick a kite. 

 ISBN 978-93-5103-601-2

2. Fill in the blanks in the story with **is**, **am** or **are**.

My name ________ Avi and I ________ Dad's helper at his restaurant today. We ________ making a special soup. Dad says his soup recipe ________ the best in town. All the ingredients ________ on Dad's kitchen counter. I ________ the one in charge of washing the vegetables and tasting the soup when it ________ ready. Dad ________ in charge of chopping the vegetables and mixing all the ingredients. We ________ a super team! Soon, the soup ________ simmering in the pot. I taste a spoonful. It ________ delicious. Now we ________ ready for our customers to arrive! I ________ very excited!

Remember!

- We use **is** with singular nouns and the pronouns **he**, **she** and **it**, e.g. The eagle **is** a bird of prey.
- We use **are** with plural nouns and the pronouns **you**, **we** and **they**, e.g. Dolphins **are** friendly animals.
- We use **am** when we are talking about ourselves, e.g. I **am** seven years old.

3. Fill in each blank with **is**, **am** or **are** and the **-ing** form of the **verb** given in the brackets.

   a. I ____________ (mend) my shoes.
   b. The gardener ____________ (water) the plants.
   c. The aircraft ____________ (fly) through thick clouds.
   d. The Sinhas ____________ (visit) their daughter in Australia.
   e. The children ____________ (listen) to a radio programme.

4. Complete the sentences using **is**, **am** or **are** and an **-ing verb**. The pictures will help you.

   a.  I ____________ a book.

   b.  Dad ____________ to the office.

   c. 

Rex ____________ water from his favourite bowl.

   d.  We ____________ the national anthem.

   e.  The cows ____________ in the field.

 ISBN 978-93-5103-601-2

5. Fill in each blank with **was** or **were**.

a. Twenty years ago, this area ________ a farm.

b. Jo and I ________ friends at school.

c. Long ago, people believed dragons ________ real.

d. It ________ late when Dad came home from the airport.

e. I put on some sunscreen because the sun ________ so hot.

f. We ________ outside in the garden when the phone rang.

6. Circle the correct **verb** to complete each sentence.

a. Sonal (was / were) upset when I spilt juice on her dress.

b. Mia and I (was / were) in the park when it began to rain.

c. The paint (was / were) still wet when I checked this morning.

d. Years ago, there (was / were) an earthquake that destroyed the city.

e. The children (was / were) delighted because it was the last day of school.

7. Fill in the blanks in the story with **was** or **were**. The picture will help you.

There ________ a tennis tournament at school today. We ________ very excited. The match ________ between our two top tennis players. It ________ a close match. There ________ loud cheers when it ended. The winner ________ very happy. The chief guest awarded her the trophy. It ________ huge and beautiful. There ________ many parents in the stands. They clapped loudly.

 ISBN 978-93-5103-601-2

8. Fill in each blank with **has**, **have** or **had**.

a. Grandmother ________ a hearing aid to help her hear better.

b. Kriti ________ a party at her house yesterday.

c. We reached home late, so we ________ pizza for dinner.

d. You ________ a talent for drawing animals.

e. Our music teacher ________ a sore throat last week.

f. Carnivores ________ sharp teeth to catch and eat their prey.

Remember!

- We use **have** with plural nouns and the pronouns **I**, **we**, **you** and **they**.
- We use **has** with singular nouns and the pronouns **he**, **she** and **it**.

9. Look at the picture below. Write three sentences about it using **has** and **have**.

____

____

____

____

____

10. Circle the correct **simple present tense** form to complete each sentence.

a. Tim (knock / knocks) on the door.

b. The stuntwomen (jump / jumps) into the river.

c. Pia and her sister (win / wins) the game.

d. Ishaan (lock / locks) his diary in the drawer.

e. The boys (eat / eats) oranges.

11. Fill in the **simple past tense** form of each **verb**.

	Verb	Simple past tense
a.	climb	
b.	close	
c.	push	
d.	rain	
e.	waste	

 ISBN 978-93-5103-601-2

5.2 There is, there are

Read the story.

"**There is** half an hour before your bus arrives. I'll pack you a cucumber-and-cheese sandwich," Mum tells Ben.

"**There is** no cheese, Mum," says Ben, "but **there are** plenty of tomatoes."

"I'll make salad then," says Mum. "**There is** a fork in the top drawer. Please pass it to me."

Why do you think Mum needs the fork?

How much time is left for the bus to arrive?

Why can't Mum make cucumber-and-cheese sandwiches?

What is in the top drawer?

1. Look at the pictures above. Then circle the suitable words to complete each sentence.
   a. (There is / There are) two people in the kitchen.
   b. (There is / There are) a loaf of bread on the table.
   c. (There is / There are) vegetables in the fridge.

2. Write each sentence ending from the box in the correct column below.

a pond near the palace.	many tourists at the hotel.
raindrops on the grass.	an apple in the bowl.
mosquitoes in the garden.	

There is ...	There are ...

We use the words **there is** and **there are** to talk about things that exist around us, or things we know about.

 ISBN 978-93-5103-601-2

Let's Practise

A. Look at the picture below. Complete the sentences to describe it.

Take Note
We use **there is** with a singular noun and **there are** with a plural noun.

1. There is ______________________________
2. There are ______________________________
3. There is ______________________________
4. There are ______________________________
5. There is ______________________________
6. There are ______________________________

B. Match the columns to make sentences. Write the sentences below.

Column A	Column B
There is	three men in the boat.
	a bucket near the door.
There are	one cookie left in the jar.
	many boxes under your bed.
	a cat on the roof.

1. ______________________________
2. ______________________________
3. ______________________________
4. ______________________________
5. ______________________________

 ISBN 978-93-5103-601-2

5.3 Simple present tense

Read the story.

Sam **lives** in a very hot city. The sun **shines** brightly every day. It **makes** Sam sweat.

Every summer, Sam **paints** the door of his garage. The hot sun **makes** the paint dry fast.

Sam's neighbours **go** to the local department store every week. They **smile** whenever they see him.

Remember!
We use the simple present tense to talk about things as they happen.

Do you think Sam's neighbours are friendly people? Why do you think so?

What does the sun do every day?

Why does the paint dry fast?

What do Sam's neighbours do whenever they see him?

1. Fill in each blank with a verb from the story above.
   a. Working in the hot sun every day __________ Sam sweat.
   b. Sam __________ his entire house every year.
   c. Sam's neighbours __________ to Hawaii every winter.

2. Underline the verb in each sentence below.
   a. Akshay eats noodles every week.
   b. Raj drinks milk in the morning.
   c. Birds fly south for the winter.
   d. Wolves hunt their prey in packs.
   e. Our book club meets every Tuesday.
   f. Water freezes when the temperature is very low.
   g. The milkman delivers the milk at eight o'clock.
   h. I polish my shoes at night.

We use the **simple present tense** for actions that happen regularly. We also use it to talk about things that are true now and will always be true.

 ISBN 978-93-5103-601-2

Let's Practise

A. Fill in each blank with the **simple present tense** of the verbs given in the box below.

walk	dig	flow	ask	buy

1. Earthworms __________ tunnels in the soil.
2. Dad __________ fruit from the vendor in the market.
3. Water __________ from a higher level to a lower level.
4. Mum __________ me to wear a jacket when it's windy.
5. Grandfather __________ slowly with his walking stick to the park every evening.

Take Note
The simplest form of a verb is called its **base form**, e.g. **go**, **like**, **play**.

Remember!
We usually add **-s** to the verbs when we talk about singular nouns.

B. Complete the crossword with verbs in the **simple present tense**. The clues given below will help you.

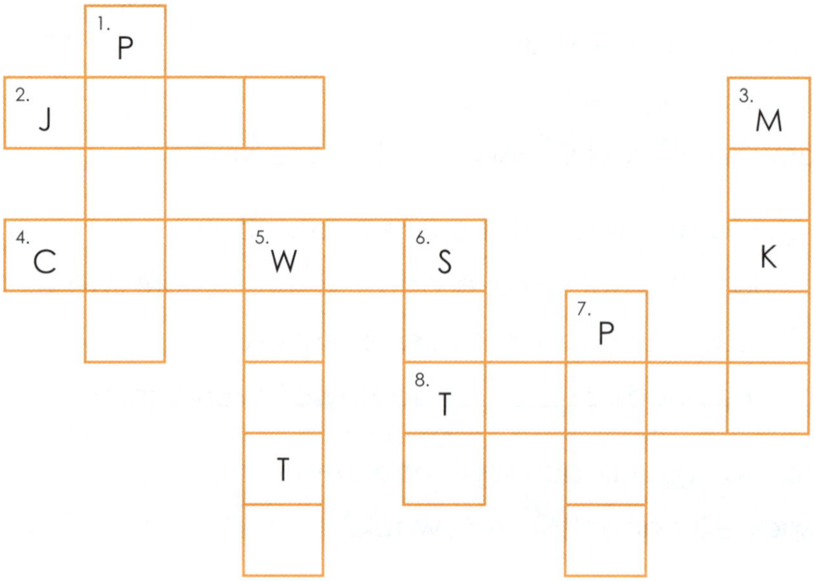

Across

2. Raman _____ in the park every evening to stay fit.
4. The turtle _____ on land.
8. Dad _____ us to brush our teeth twice daily.

Down

1. Mrs Arora _____ out juice for herself every morning.
3. Rahim _____ gifts for all his friends.
5. Alisha _____ for her father near the school gate every day.
6. A mother bird _____ on her eggs to make them hatch.
7. Sheena's dogs _____ with cats!

 ISBN 978-93-5103-601-2

5.4 Simple past tense

Read the story.

Ruby and Dad **went** on a hot-air-balloon ride. The pilot **told** them to follow the safety instructions.

The balloon **began** to lift into the air. Soon, it **rose** high above the ground.

Ruby and Dad **saw** the houses below. "The houses look so small!" **said** Ruby with delight.

Remember!
We use the simple past tense to talk about things that happened in the past, e.g. The train **arrived** early in the morning.

What else do you think Ruby and Dad saw from the balloon?

Where did Ruby and Dad go?

What happened after the balloon lifted into the air?

What did Ruby and Dad see?

1. Replace each underlined verb with a suitable verb from the story above.

   On Sunday, Dad tells Ruby about hot-air balloons. Ruby and Dad then go on a hot-air-balloon ride. The pilot begins to take the balloon up into the air. As the balloon rises, Ruby sees the houses getting smaller and smaller. "This is such fun!"she says.

2. Fill in each blank with a verb from the box below.

made	broke	spoke	lost	wrote

a. The vase ________ because it got knocked over by the wind.

b. Pat ________ a letter to her cousin in India.

c. The cat ________ no sound as it crept into the room.

d. We thought we were ________ but Chen knew the way.

e. Ali ________ to his coach yesterday.

The **simple past tense** form of some verbs does not end in **-d** or **-ed** but is quite different from the base form.

 ISBN 978-93-5103-601-2

Let's Practise

A. Circle the correct **verb** to complete each sentence.

1. Dhruv (wake / woke) up at midnight to see the lunar eclipse.
2. My brother (teach / taught) me how to tie my shoelaces.
3. Suresh slipped and (fell / fall) down the stairs.
4. Irom (sent / send) a parcel to her mother last week.
5. Mum (drive / drove) us to the museum.

B. Circle the correct **simple past tense** form of the verbs given below.

1.	buy	buyed	bought
2.	eat	ate	eated
3.	fly	flyed	flew
4.	sell	selled	sold
5.	break	breaked	broke
6.	hear	heard	heared
7.	bend	bent	bended
8.	drink	drinked	drank
9.	tear	teared	tore
10.	build	built	builded

C. In the grid below, find the **simple past tense** form of the verbs given in the box.

find run draw sit blow sing think meet

J	Q	L	C	U	F	O	U	N	D
Y	V	O	M	A	B	I	C	V	G
O	P	M	J	P	Y	H	P	S	Q
B	L	E	W	H	J	Q	M	A	U
H	I	T	H	O	U	G	H	T	H
R	C	U	G	L	I	L	J	Y	L
A	M	Q	Y	P	M	D	R	E	W
N	L	S	A	N	G	V	U	I	P

 ISBN 978-93-5103-601-2

5.5 Simple future tense

Read the story.

"There **will be** a long queue at the cashier, Pedro," said Mum. "So let's finish shopping quickly."

"I **shall need** some fish for a curry dish," said Mum. "**Will** you **make** roast potato too?"asked Pedro.

"Yes, dear," said Mum. "Your friends **will like** that, I know."

What do you think Mum and Pedro are shopping for?

Why does Mum want to finish shopping quickly?

What does Pedro ask Mum?

Why does Mum want to make roast potato?

1. Fill in the blanks with verbs from the story above.

   "Today is my birthday!" says Pedro happily. "All my friends ________ at the party tonight. There ________ a magician too. He knows many tricks that my friends ________. Mum ________ fish curry and roast potato for dinner. My friends ________ that! They love Mum's cooking."

2. Read the sentences below. Underline the verbs that show that something will happen in the future.

   a. I shall go to the supermarket on Saturday.
   b. India will play Sri Lanka in the final match.
   c. Shubha's parents will meet the class teacher after school.
   d. Kavya will watch the cookery show this afternoon.
   e. We shall attend the seminar next week.
   f. You will win the race tomorrow if you practise hard.

We use the **simple future tense** to talk about things that will happen in the future. We use the verbs **will** and **shall** as helping verbs with the main verbs to form the simple future tense.

 ISBN 978-93-5103-601-2

Let's Practise

A. Make a sentence using the **simple future tense** with each group of words given below. The picture will help you.

> **Take Note**
> We use the helping verb **shall** with the pronouns **I** and **we**, and the helping verb **will** with all nouns and the pronouns **you**, **he**, **she**, **it** and **they**.

1. Anita Tokyo next month 

____

2. Meena the next race 

____

3. Dad favourite blue suit Nisha's wedding 

____

4. I friend postcard from Italy 

____

5. Our teacher us museum next week 

____

B. Replace the underlined verb in each sentence with a verb in the **simple future tense**. Rewrite the new sentence in the blank below.

1. Rahul <u>went</u> to the market to buy a pair of boots.

____

2. The school <u>closed</u> for the summer holidays.

____

3. Sania <u>plays</u> with her new neighbours in the evening.

____

4. We <u>visited</u> the science museum today.

____

Think & Share Divide the class into groups. Create posters about the annual school fair. Each group should write five sentences about different activities and stalls that will be at the fair, using the words **will** and **shall**. Display your posters in class.

 ISBN 978-93-5103-601-2

5.6 Present continuous tense

Read the story.

Joe **is leaving** for work early today. "Oh no! It **is raining** again!" he exclaims.

"Shall I bring your umbrella?" asks Mona. "No, I **am wearing** my raincoat," replies Joe.

"I **am rushing** for an early appointment. I don't want to be late!" says Joe.

Do you think Joe will get wet in the rain? Why do you think so?

What is Joe doing in the first picture?

What is Joe wearing to protect himself from the rain?

Why is Joe getting ready so early in the morning?

1. Look at the pictures above. Then fill in the blanks with verbs that show something is happening now.

It ________ outside. Joe ________ ready to go to work. He ________ on his raincoat and boots. He ________ to work as he has an early-morning meeting. Mona is in the kitchen. She ________ Joe's lunch. Joe ________ towards the door. Mona ________ goodbye to him.

2. Rewrite each sentence below to show that the action is happening now.

a. The tailor mends Salim's ripped jeans.

____

b. I climb up the ladder in the garage.

____

c. Rustam works in the garden.

____

d. My sisters watch the news on television.

____

e. Venkat helps me complete my assignments.

____

f. I clean my desk and cupboard.

____

We use the **present continuous tense** to show actions that are happening now. We use the verbs **is**, **am** and **are** as helping verbs with the **-ing** form of the main verbs to form the present continuous tense.

 ISBN 978-93-5103-601-2

Let's Practise

A. Tick the correct form of the **verb** to complete each sentence.

1. I _____ to my favourite song.
   a. am listening b. is listening
2. The team _____ for the next match.
   a. am preparing b. is preparing
3. Baljeet _____ an adventure story.
   a. are reading b. is reading
4. The teachers _____ a meeting.
   a. are attending b. am attending

B. Fill in the missing form of the **verb**.

	Verb	Present continuous form
1.	clap	He __________.
2.	dress	We __________.
3.	look	They __________.
4.	point	I __________.
5.	snow	It __________.

C. Complete the story using the **present continuous tense** of the verbs given in the brackets.

Our class __________ (work) on a garden project. We __________ (make) a small garden outside our class window. Sanya and Max __________ (tidy) up the area. They __________ (pick) up the trash people have dropped there. Vinnie __________ (clear) away the collected trash. Amu and Pooja __________ (dig) the soil. Adi __________ (sow) some fruit and flower seeds. I __________ (make) a scarecrow to keep birds away. Our teacher __________ (take) photos of our project.

 ISBN 978-93-5103-601-2

5.7 Past continuous tense

Read the story.

Last night, Sasha **was studying** for an exam. Soon, she **was yawning** so much, she decided to go to bed.

The neighbours **were having** a party. They **were making** so much noise, she could not sleep!

Sasha **was trying** to read a book, but the noise **was driving** her crazy!

How do you think Sasha felt the next morning?

Why did Sasha decide to go to bed?

Why couldn't she sleep?

Why couldn't she read her book?

1. Look at the pictures above. Then circle the suitable verbs to complete the story.

   Sasha (were trying / was trying) to study, but she felt too sleepy. She couldn't sleep because her neighbours (was having / were having) a party. They (were playing / was playing) loud music. Some people (was dancing / were dancing) too. Sasha tried to read, but the music was too loud.

2. Tick the sentences that talk about something that was taking place in the past.

   a. The principal talks to the students in the playground. ☐
   b. The dentist was checking my sister's teeth. ☐
   c. People were waiting for the traffic light to turn green. ☐
   d. I am packing my suitcase for my holiday in Goa. ☐
   e. Children were flying kites in the gentle breeze. ☐
   f. Sid was baking cupcakes in the kitchen. ☐

We use the **past continuous tense** to talk about something that was happening at a certain time in the past. We use the verbs **was** and **were** as helping verbs with the **-ing** form of the main verbs to form the past continuous tense.

 ISBN 978-93-5103-601-2

Let's Practise

A. Fill in each blank with the **past continuous tense** of the verb given in the brackets.

Remember!
Was and **were** are also used as main verbs.

1. The chef ______________ (prepare) the dish of the day.
2. Meera ______________ (work) on the computer this morning.
3. The children ______________ (walk) home when it began to rain.
4. The birds ______________ (chirp) long before my alarm rang.
5. At this time last Friday, I ______________ (talk) to Anna on the phone.

B. Make sentences using the **past continuous tense** to say what Pete the Panda was doing yesterday. The pictures will help you.

1.  ____
2.  ____
3.  ____
4.  ____
5.  ____

C. Make sentences using the **past continuous tense** about what any two of your friends or classmates were doing together at the times given below.

1. 9 a.m. yesterday
____
2. lunchtime last Sunday
____
3. yesterday evening
____
4. this morning
____
5. an hour ago
____

 ISBN 978-93-5103-601-2

5.8 Can, may

Read the story.

Ted is bored. "I **can** watch TV or I **can** play on the computer," he thinks.

"Hi Ted! **May** I watch the cricket match with you?" asks Pete. "Yes, we **can** watch it together," says Ted.

"It **may** rain though. We **can** play chess if the match is cancelled," says Pete.

Do you think that Ted is still bored at the end of the story?

What does Ted think of doing when he is bored?

What does Pete ask Ted?

Why does Pete think the match could get cancelled?

1. Fill in the blanks with suitable words from the story above.

   a. Ted ________ think of nothing interesting to do.

   b. "________ I watch TV with you?" asks Pete. "Yes, of course you ________," replies Ted.

   c. Rain ________ delay the match.

   d. Ted and Pete ________ play chess together.

2. Match the columns to make a complete sentence.

a.	My dog	i.	may address the crowd today.
b.	A shark	ii.	I borrow your ladder?
c.	The minister	iii.	can jump over the neighbour's fence.
d.	I	iv.	may join our club.
e.	May	v.	can swim fast to catch its prey.
f.	The new boy	vi.	can cook a yummy pasta dish.

We use the verb **can** to show someone is able to do something. We use the verb **may** to ask for or give permission to do something. We also use the words **may** and **can** to talk about things that are possible or could happen.

 ISBN 978-93-5103-601-2

Let's Practise

A. Make a sentence using the verb **can** and each group of words given below.

1. help homework

____

2. storm damage

____

3. pack bag

____

4. cheetah run hyena

____

B. Write a sentence for each picture using the verb **may**.

1. 

____

2. 
____

3. 
____

4. 
____

C. Fill in the blanks with **can** or **may**.

1. Anirudh ________ make wooden toys.
2. ________ you play the piano?
3. Mr Sen, please ________ I borrow your pen?
4. I'm not sure but Avi ________ come to the party today.
5. Farida is a programmer. She ________ design computer programs.

Think & Share Play the "I can" game with your classmates. Make a set of cards with amusing activities written on them, for example, Touch your nose with your tongue. Each classmate picks a card and reads out the activity. Whoever can perform that activity must raise their hand and say, "I can" and then show the class. The person who can perform the most activities wins the game.

 ISBN 978-93-5103-601-2

6 Adverbs

Let's Recall

- **How words** describe the way an action is done. Such words are called **adverbs**. An adverb describes or tells us more about a verb.
- Some adverbs tell us **how** something is done. They are usually formed by adding **-ly** to adjectives, for example, The cheetah ran **swiftly**.

6.1 Revising adverbs

1. Write a sentence using the **-ly** form of each word given below. The picture will help you.

a.  loud ______________________________

b.  careful ______________________________

c.  brave ______________________________

d.  happy ______________________________

2. Tick the correct **adverb** to complete the sentence.

a. People must speak _____ in the library.
   i. softly   ii. sadly   iii. quickly

b. The giant laughed _____ when he saw the little boy.
   i. carefully   ii. loudly   iii. nervously

c. Beth walked _____ to the bus stop because she was late.
   i. quickly   ii. slowly   iii. silently

d. Mike held the handles of his bicycle _____.
   i. kindly   ii. warmly   iii. tightly

Take Note

- An adverb is usually placed after the verb it is describing, e.g. The teacher spoke **sternly** to the children.
- An adverb can also be placed away from the verb, e.g. The teacher spoke to the children **sternly**.

 ISBN 978-93-5103-601-2

6.2 More about adverbs (1)

Read the story.

What game are Roger and Peter playing?

Where is the crowd watching the match from?

What does Peter do?

Where does Peter move to reach the ball?

1. Fill in each blank with a suitable word from the story above.

    a. We can hear loud sounds coming from the flat ________.

    b. A herd of deer were standing quite ________.

    c. I was at the beach and I think I dropped my keys ________.

2. Fill in each blank with a word from the box below that shows the place of action.

here	there	near	behind	below	above

    a. A jet plane flew across the sky with white clouds trailing ________.

    b. This is my school. I like studying ________.

    c. When we looked up, we saw eagles flying ________.

    d. A rumbling sound told us that the train was getting ________.

    e. I love going to the park with my friends, so I can play ________.

    f. The jackal tumbled downhill and landed in the bushes ________.

Adverbs such as **above**, **below**, **here**, **there**, **near** and **behind** tell us where something happens.

 ISBN 978-93-5103-601-2

Let's Practise

A. Circle the correct **adverb** to complete the sentence.

1. Girish stood below the tree and looked at the stars (above / near).
2. My cousin lives in Nairobi with her daughter. I have never been (there / here).
3. There is a park behind our house. My brother plays football (there / here).
4. We knew the house was somewhere (near / above).
5. They picked up their bags and walked to the valley (near / below).
6. This is my favourite restaurant. I love the sundaes they serve (there / here).
7. Mary walked to school and the little lamb followed (here / behind).
8. The ball bounced and landed in the field (below / above).

Take Note
When we use **above**, **below**, **here**, **there**, **near** and **behind** as adverbs, we do not add a noun or pronoun after them.

B. Look at the picture. Make sentences describing it using the **adverbs** given below.

1. above

____

2. here

____

3. there

____

4. near

____

5. behind

____

 ISBN 978-93-5103-601-2

6.3 More about adverbs (2)

Read the story.

Dad called from London **yesterday**. He was attending a conference there.

Dad is coming home **today**. His flight is late.

Dad brought chocolates for me! I will share them with my friends **tomorrow**!

Is the boy a good friend? Why do you think so?

When did Dad call from London?

When is Dad arriving?

When will the boy share his chocolates with his friends?

1. Fill in the blanks with words from the story above.

   "Hi, Dad, when are you coming home?" I asked.

   "I'll be back ________," said Dad. "I'm going to the mall ________ to get some gifts for you all. I didn't get any time to shop ________."

   "Great! We'll be at the airport ________ to pick you up," I said.

2. Complete each sentence with a word that shows the time of an action. You may use some words more than once.

   a. Mia is late for band practice ________.

   b. It was a holiday ________ but we have to work today.

   c. I am very busy right now. Let's get together ________.

   d. Anil woke up early ________, so he is ready for school now.

   e. Arti attended the meeting ________ though she was unwell.

   f. Eva went to meet Uma ________ but she wasn't at home.

Adverbs such as **yesterday**, **today** and **tomorrow** tell us when something happens.

 ISBN 978-93-5103-601-2

Let's Practise

A. Rewrite each sentence using the **adverb(s)** given in the brackets.

1. My sister arrived from Kolkata. (yesterday)

   ____

2. The prime minister will give a speech. (tomorrow)

   ____

3. The weather forecast predicts heavy rain. (today)

   ____

4. My dog found a bone in the garden. (yesterday)

   ____

5. Mum is going to pick me up from school early. (today)

   ____

6. I started reading a new novel and finished it. (yesterday/today)

   ____

B. Make a sentence using the adverb **today**, **tomorrow** or **yesterday**, and the words given below. Use each **adverb** at least once.

1. wrap present

   ____

2. horse jumped fence

   ____

3. holiday Eid

   ____

Think & Share Play the Adverb game. Form three teams called **Yesterday**, **Today** and **Tomorrow**. Each team gets a list of ten verbs and the members have to make sentences with the verbs that must include their team's adverb, for example, I baked a cake today. The team that finishes making ten correct sentences first wins the game.

 ISBN 978-93-5103-601-2

Review 2

1. Underline the **adjective** in each sentence. Then write in the blank what **kind of adjective** it is. Choose from the kinds given in the box below.

material	appearance	age	speed	temperature	quality

a. Shruti likes driving fast cars. ________

b. The ancient monuments of Rome attract tourists even today. ________

c. We used soft cheese to make the sandwiches. ________

d. Dad bought a beautiful cover for the sofa. ________

e. Pete pulled on a jumper as the icy wind swirled around him. ________

f. The Science teacher asked us to bring plastic containers for an experiment. ________

2. Unscramble the letters to form **adjectives** and complete each sentence.

a. There were ________ (namy) ants on the honey jar.

b. Eating too ________ (cuhm) sugar can cause tooth decay.

c. Vikas asked me to buy ________ (mose) butter from the supermarket.

d. Anne put a ________ (liltet) glue on the picture and stuck it in her diary.

3. Fill in the blanks below with the **adjective** and the noun it describes in each sentence.

	Adjective	**Noun it describes**
a. These pyjamas need to be ironed.	________	________
b. This diary belongs to Sadia.	________	________
c. James lives in that house at the end of the lane.	________	________
d. Those plants have to be watered as they are drying up.	________	________
e. Dad bought these vegetables from the grocer.	________	________
f. Sarabjeet left the brochures on that table.	________	________

 ISBN 978-93-5103-601-2

4. Add **-est** or **most** to each **adjective** given below.

	Adjective	Form of comparison
a.	amazing	
b.	beautiful	
c.	deadly	
d.	fast	
e.	friendly	
f.	happy	
g.	loud	
h.	popular	
i.	pretty	
j.	strange	

5. Circle the correct words to complete each sentence.

a. (There is / There are) a peacock in the garden.
b. (There is / There are) a banana left in the fruit bowl.
c. (There is / There are) many people waiting in the queue.
d. (There is / There are) mosquitoes coming in through the window.
e. (There is / There are) an article about the earthquake in the newspaper.

6. Fill in each blank with the **simple present tense** of the verb given in the brackets.

a. Anjali ________ (write) in her diary every night.
b. My brother ________ (play) the French horn every Friday.
c. I ________ (wake) up in the morning when I hear the birds chirping.
d. Dad ________ (listen) to classical music on his radio in the evening.
e. The waves ________ (splash) against the rocks when the tide is high.

7. Fill in each blank with a suitable verb in the **simple past tense** from the box below.

drew	heard	sold	broke	wept

a. The king ________ when he heard the sad tale of the old woman.
b. Darla's little brother ________ all over the newly painted walls in his room.
c. Sam's pencil ________ when he pressed down too hard on the paper.
d. The Mehta family ________ their house in the city and moved to their farm.
e. Sana ________ a strange creaking sound in the middle of the night.

 ISBN 978-93-5103-601-2

8. Rewrite each sentence to show the action will happen in the **future**.

a. They visit their cousins during the winter vacation.

____

b. I take my paintbrushes to the art class on Monday.

____

c. I go to the doctor only for major illnesses.

____

d. Anita plays chess with her father on Sunday.

____

e. The mother bird gets some worms for the hungry chicks.

____

9. Circle the **present tense verbs**, underline the **past tense verbs** and double-underline the **future tense verbs**.

jogged	hopped	share	woke	laughed	shall help
will try	shout	cried	dances	washes	will grow
will throw	ran	shopped	eat	will walk	liked
sneezed	look	will sing	played	carry	will paint

10. Write a sentence using each group of words given below. Use the **present continuous tense** of the verb.

a. Savita help mother

____

b. Praful laugh at clown

____

c. Goldfish swim in bowl

____

d. Nita sing favourite song

____

e. Nitesh come to fair

____

11. Fill in the blanks with the **past continuous tense** of the verb in the brackets.

a. The baby ______________ (play) in her cot.

b. The astronaut ______________ (prepare) for her space mission.

c. Dad ______________ (work) on a business presentation till late last night.

 ISBN 978-93-5103-601-2

d. We ____________ (walk) home from the park yesterday when the storm broke.

e. Reporters ____________ (ask) the chief minister about his plans for the city at the news conference.

12. Fill in each blank with **can** or **may**.

a. ________ I use your book?

b. Piya ________ ride a horse.

c. It ________ rain tomorrow.

d. My little sister ________ count till ten.

e. I think Susie ________ go to the planetarium today.

13. Underline the **adverbs** that show where or when an action takes place.

a. I saw Mani at the station and wondered what he was doing there.

b. Above, aircraft were crossing the sky in all directions.

c. We are going on a school trip to the ice-cream factory today.

d. I stayed behind and finished my work.

e. Come here and taste the soup I've made.

f. They couldn't attend the opening ceremony yesterday.

g. Jamil came up on deck and then disappeared below.

h. The sound of a band meant the procession was getting near.

i. Mrs Singh will test our spelling tomorrow.

Spot the Error

14. There is a mistake in each sentence. Underline it and rewrite the sentence correctly in the blank below.

a. There isn't many coffee left in my cup.

____

b. The black mamba is one of the dangerousest snakes in the world.

____

c. There is many ancient forts in Agra for tourists to visit.

____

d. Meghna's dog wag its tail when she comes home in the afternoon.

____

e. Adya could not sleep last night because her father snore loudly.

____

f. My little brother went to the market tomorrow.

____

 ISBN 978-93-5103-601-2

7 Prepositions

Let's Recall
Where words such as **at**, **by**, **from**, **over**, **into** and **behind** tell us where someone or something is in relation to another person or thing, or a place. They are called **prepositions**.

7.1 Revising prepositions

1. Circle the correct **preposition** to complete each sentence. The picture will help you.

Take Note
Prepositions are usually followed by nouns or pronouns.

a. Dimple jumped (into / over)  the puddle.

b. Leo is hiding (over / behind)  the curtain.

c. The party was held (at / by)  Kamal's house.

d. Virat returned (from / behind)  the market an hour ago.

e. I was surprised to see the dog jump (into / over)  the water.

2. Underline the **preposition** in the sentences below.

a. Jean is standing behind Helen.

b. The birds flew over the chimney.

c. My mother likes travelling by train.

d. Sandy received a gift from his brother.

e. I will meet you at the coffee shop.

 ISBN 978-93-5103-601-2

7.2 More about prepositions

Read the story.

There is a river **between** the new and old parts of our city. It flows **to** the ocean. Yesterday, Dad took us **for** a boat ride **in** the afternoon.

We went **around** the river twice, then stopped **for** lunch. We saw a seagull flying **above** us.

Suddenly, it dived **through** the air. It had found its lunch too!

What was the seagull's lunch?

Where does the river flow?

Where was the seagull flying?

Where did the seagull dive?

1. Fill in each blank with a suitable word from the story above.

   a. Pooja will buy a gift ________ her mother.

   b. Shane sits ________ his two best friends in class.

   c. We like to walk ________ a new city to explore it.

   d. The kitten squeezed ________ the fence.

   e. Sumeet will go home ________ the evening.

2. Match the columns to complete the sentences.

a.	The mechanic drove the car	•	•	i.	of the year.
b.	Abha enjoys walking	•	•	ii.	to the workshop.
c.	June is the sixth month	•	•	iii.	on Sunday.
d.	The exam will start	•	•	iv.	before bedtime.
e.	We shall go for a picnic	•	•	v.	around her garden.
f.	Drink your milk	•	•	vi.	at ten o'clock.

Some **prepositions** show us the connection of a person or thing with a place (where) and some prepositions show us the connection of a happening with a time (when).

 ISBN 978-93-5103-601-2

Let's Practise

A. Fill in the blanks with **prepositions**.

before	for	through	in	across
on	at	after	to	between

1. Cindy walked ________ the forest.
2. They will watch the film ________ Saturday.
3. The train will leave ________ the evening.
4. The girl ran swiftly ________ the field.
5. He eats too many sweets ________ meals.
6. The programme will start ________ five o'clock sharp.
7. We must wash our hands ________ and ________ each meal.
8. The Bamjees went ________ Africa ________ their summer vacation.

B. Underline the incorrect **preposition** in each sentence below. Rewrite the sentence correctly.

1. The farmer put a wooden fence to his land.

____

2. I went around the meeting wearing my favourite coat.

____

3. People must turn off their mobile phones through the film.

____

4. The group sang a traditional song at us.

____

5. The mouse entered during the window.

____

Think & Share Pair up with a classmate. Write six prepositions on different slips of paper and put them in a bowl. Draw six different activities on another six slips of paper and put them in another bowl. Take turns to pick a slip of paper from each bowl and make a sentence which uses both the preposition and the activity.

 ISBN 978-93-5103-601-2

8 Conjunctions

Let's Recall

- **Joining words** such as **and**, **or** and **but** can be used to join words, groups of words or sentences together. Joining words are called **conjunctions**.
- We use **but** to join words, groups of words or sentences that have different or opposite meanings.
- We use **or** to join words, groups of words or sentences that show choice between two or more options.

8.1 Revising conjunctions

1. Fill in each blank with **and**, **or** or **but**.

   a. I want to study medicine ________ train as a doctor.

   b. The weather will be mostly calm ________ very sunny today.

   c. Shall I play a computer game ________ watch a film?

   d. The plant is attractive to look at ________ very poisonous.

   e. Today Mum had no time to comb her hair ________ put on her make-up.

   f. Dad is impressed by my computer skills ________ shocked at my handwriting.

2. Fill in the blanks with the help of the pictures. Then join the sentences using **and**, **or** or **but**.

   a. Mina likes the colour ________ . Mina likes the colour ________ 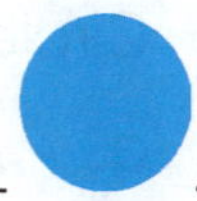.

   ____

   b. Did you order ________ ? Did you order ________ 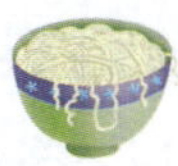?

   ____

   c. I have a pet ________ . I don't have a pet ________ .

   ____

 ISBN 978-93-5103-601-2

8.2 More about conjunctions

Read the story.

Mr Verma often ate unhealthy food in his office, **though** he knew it was not good for him.

He struggled on the stairs **because** he had put on a lot of weight.

Mr Verma wanted to get fit, **so** he joined a gym.

What is unhealthy food? Do you eat unhealthy food?

What harmful habit did Mr Verma have?

Why did he struggle on the staircase?

Why did he decide to join a gym?

1. Fill in each blank with a word from the story above. Then match the columns to complete the sentences.

a.	Mr Verma had difficulty climbing the stairs •	• i.	________ he knew it was bad for him.
b.	Mr Verma liked eating unhealthy food •	• ii.	________ he started exercising regularly.
c.	Mr Verma wanted to be healthy •	• iii.	________ he was overweight.

2. Circle the correct conjunction to complete each sentence.

   a. Anu packed her raincoat (because / though) it was not likely to rain.

   b. I invited Vani for my birthday (because / though) she is my best friend.

   c. Mrs Mehra had toothache (though / so) she went to the dentist.

   d. Dad is very tired today (so / because) he worked till late last night.

   e. Alex couldn't reach the shelf (though / so) he is quite tall.

   f. Gloria was late for the film (because / so) she watched a play instead.

The words **so**, **because** and **though** are also **conjunctions**. These words are often used to join sentences together.

 ISBN 978-93-5103-601-2

Let's Practise

A. Tick the correct **conjunction** to complete each sentence.

		so	because	though
1.	We mustn't be late for the concert, ____ pick me up early.	☐	☐	☐
2.	Pat cannot go to work ____ she has flu.	☐	☐	☐
3.	Anup ate a pie ____ he said he wasn't hungry.	☐	☐	☐
4.	Geet was upset ____ she had missed her train.	☐	☐	☐
5.	I don't really know Mika ____ we are next-door neighbours.	☐	☐	☐

B. Complete each sentence using **so**, **because** or **though**. Use each **conjunction** at least once.

1. Vidhi came with us ________________________________.
2. We should always recycle waste ________________________________.
3. Fruit has vitamins and minerals ________________________________.
4. I would like to become a firefighter ________________________________.
5. The wind is blowing ________________________________.

C. Complete each sentence with the help of the picture.

1.  ____________________ so she did not participate in the talent show.

2.  ______________________________ because his mother asked him to.

3.  ____ though it tastes bitter.

4.  ______________________________ because it is her sister's birthday.

Think & Share Get into two teams. Each team writes 20 sentences on slips of paper and places them in a basket. Then each member has to pick one slip from each team's basket and combine the sentences using the conjunctions **so**, **because** or **though**.

 ISBN 978-93-5103-601-2

9 Sentences

Let's Recall

- A **sentence** is a group of words that makes complete sense.
- A sentence begins with a capital letter and usually ends with a full stop.
- A sentence has a **naming part** and a **doing part**.
- The naming part of a sentence is the noun, pronoun or group of words that tells us what the sentence is about. This is called its **subject**.
- The doing part of a sentence tells us something about the subject. It is called its **predicate**. The predicate contains the verb.
- The subject and the verb in a sentence must match each other.

9.1 Revising sentences

1. Tick the correct ending to complete each **sentence**.

   a. The children ________________

      i. played cricket. ii. kind. iii. the closed door.

   b. The bear is sleeping ________________

      i. sweet mangoes. ii. in the cave. iii. pink dress.

   c. Mika was painting ________________

      i. Mrs Arora's fence. ii. made of wood. iii. horse ran.

2. Rearrange each group of words to make a **sentence**. The picture will help you.

   a. 

   Shakeel eating a mango was

   ____

   b. 

   little there rain is in deserts very

   ____

   c. 

   fish in tank are two there the

   ____

 ISBN 978-93-5103-601-2

3. Fill in each blank to complete the **sentence**. Then tick the correct box to show whether your answer is the **subject** or the **predicate**.

	Subject	Predicate
a. ______________ ran because he was getting late.	☐	☐
b. How old is ______________?	☐	☐
c. Todd and Lucy ______________.	☐	☐
d. Mahatma Gandhi ______________.	☐	☐
e. This puppy ______________.	☐	☐
f. ______________ left her homework at home.	☐	☐
g. Among the tall bushes hid ______________.	☐	☐
h. ______________ wandered through the jungle.	☐	☐

Take Note

The subject can sometimes come in the second part of a sentence, e.g. Over the puddle jumped **Ollie**. Into the deep cave went **the lion**.

4. Circle the **predicate** in each sentence.

a. The baby played with the teddy bear.

b. Down the narrow path crawled the tortoise.

c. My water bottle is very colourful.

d. Where is my mobile phone?

e. The owl sat on a branch.

f. This watch is a gift from my father.

g. Out of the hat leapt a rabbit.

h. Amira watches the ducks swim.

5. Underline the **subject** in each sentence. Then circle the correct **verb** to complete the sentence.

a. The clothes (is / are) drying in the shade.

b. I (am / is) packing the cookies Mum baked.

c. Lee's grandparents (visit / visits) him once every month.

d. Today's newspaper (has / have) an interesting article on dodos.

e. Our washing machine (is / are) making a strange sound.

f. The girls (has / have) two extra uniforms.

g. Dina (plan / plans) the best parties.

h. Anna (drink / drinks) only fruit juice.

 ISBN 978-93-5103-601-2

9.2 More about sentences

Read the story.

Bess was ready for school. "Wait! **I am** looking for my school bag," **yells Ken.**

"**We shall be** late, Mum!" **complains Bess. She and Mum wait** for Ken.

Ken runs quickly downstairs. "The **bus-driver is waiting** at the gate," **says Mum.**

Did Ken find his school bag? How do you think he feels now?

Who was ready for school?

Who are going to be late for school?

What does Ken do after he finds his school bag?

1. Read the sentences in the story above. Now circle the suitable verb to complete each sentence.

   a. Bess (was / were) ready before Ken.
   b. "I (am trying / is trying) to find my bag," says Ken.
   c. Bess and Ken (is / will be) late for school!
   d. The bus-driver (is waiting / are waiting) for the children.
   e. "Hurry up, Ken!" (say / says) Mum.
   f. Ken and Bess (run / runs) to catch the bus.

2. Fill in the blanks with the suitable form of the verb(s) given in the brackets.

   a. Mum and Dad ________ together at weekends. (cook)
   b. We ________ ________ to Manali. (be, drive)
   c. The eagle ________ mice with its sharp claws. (catch)
   d. I ________ ________ my grandparents in Lucknow. (be, visit)
   e. Gina ________ to her mother every day. (talk)
   f. Sheena and Gul usually ________ in that room. (sleep)
   g. Suman ________ ________ the tree outside her window. (be, climb)
   h. Penguins ________ their wings as flippers to move through water. (use)

Remember!

The verbs **is**, **am** and **are** are forms of the verb **be**. They are often used as helping verbs with verbs that end in **-ing**.

A singular subject must have a singular verb and a plural subject must have a plural verb.

The subject and verb in a sentence must match even when the tense of the verb changes.

 ISBN 978-93-5103-601-2

Let's Practise

A. Tick the box if the **subject** matches the **verb(s)** in the sentences below.

1. Suman is climbing the tree. ☐
2. Stars shines brightly in the sky. ☐
3. My cousins was travelling to Seoul. ☐
4. The students works very hard. ☐
5. I am drawing a picture of you. ☐
6. Dogs wag their tails when they are happy. ☐
7. Mona win the race every year. ☐
8. Rajiv walks to school. ☐
9. There is horses running in the field. ☐
10. You are looking lovely today. ☐

Remember!

- We usually add **-s** to the verb when we talk about a singular subject.
- The pronoun **you** can be singular or plural, but it is always used with a plural verb.

B. Look at the picture below. Make five sentences using **singular** and **plural subjects**. Remember to match each subject to its **verb**.

____

____

____

____

____

Think & Share Play the "Matchmaker" board game with a classmate. On a large sheet of chart paper, draw 20 squares. Write a singular or plural subject (noun or pronoun) in each square. Cut a sheet of paper into 20 strips. Write a singular or plural verb on each strip. Take turns to pick a verb slip, match it to a subject and make a funny sentence. For example, Dinosaurs wear high heels.

 ISBN 978-93-5103-601-2

10 Questions

Let's Recall

- A sentence that says something is called a **statement**.
- A sentence that asks something is called a **question**.
- We often use **who**, **what**, **which**, **when**, **where**, **why** and **how** to ask for information. These are called **question words** or **wh- words**.

10.1 Revising questions

1. Complete each **question** given below. The picture will help you.

a. Do you know how ________? 

d. Are they ________? 

b. Are you a ________? 

e. Do you like ________? 

c. Is that your ________? 

f. Is Arjun your ________? 

2. Circle the correct **question word** to complete each sentence.

a. (Where / Why) is Melbourne?

b. (Who / When) is the person standing there?

c. (Why / When) does your art lesson begin?

d. (What / Who) does that sign mean?

e. (How / Which) bag is yours?

f. (How / What) did you make this pie?

3. Complete each question by adding a **question word**.

a. ________ is the shortest route to the lake?

b. ________ did you put salt in the mixture?

c. ________ many weeks are there in a year?

d. ________ is old Mrs Sahni shouting?

 ISBN 978-93-5103-601-2

4. Write a question for each answer using the **question word** given in the brackets.

a. 

I am wearing a red dress to the party. (what)

b. 

The boy talking to Sheela is her brother. (who)

c. 

That is his towel. (which)

d. 

The practice starts at three o'clock. (when)

e. 

The dancers are in the hall. (where)

f. 

Amy went to the stadium to skate. (why)

g. 

Dhiraj played the sitar beautifully. (how)

h. 

This is my laptop bag. (which)

 ISBN 978-93-5103-601-2

10.2 Forming questions

Read the story.

"**Is** the kite stuck?" asks Dad. "**Are** you going to climb the tree?" asks Mum.

Crack! "**Was** that the sound of the branch breaking?" asks Dad.

"**Are** you badly hurt, Dad? **Is** there something I can do for you?" asks Andy.

What do you think Dad replies to Andy? Who will help him?

What does Mum ask Dad?

What does Dad ask when he hears a sound?

What does Andy ask Dad?

1. Read the story again. Write a question for each answer below.

   a. ______________________________

      The kite is stuck.

   b. ______________________________

      That was the sound of the branch breaking.

   c. ______________________________

      Dad was badly hurt.

2. Rearrange each statement below to form a question.

   a. This ice cream is home-made. ______________________

   b. You are working late. ______________________

   c. I am driving too fast. ______________________

   d. Sam was sleeping outside. ______________________

   e. There are many trees in the orchard. ______________________

When we form a **question**, we usually change the order of the words and place the verb first, for example, **Is** she an astronaut?

 ISBN 978-93-5103-601-2

Let's Practise

A. Write a **question** for each answer below.

Remember!
We use the words **there is** and **there are** to talk about things that exist around us, or things we know about.

1. 

____

I am singing loudly.

2. 

____

There is a hole in my cardigan.

3. 

____

The pizza was baked in the oven.

4. 

____

We were happy to go to Egypt.

5. 

____

There are cookies in the tin.

6. 

____

The farmer was looking for his sheep.

B. Rearrange each group of words below to form a **question**.

1. Dave late for is school ______________________________
2. the talking boys were ______________________________
3. pass exam am going I to the ______________________________
4. apple bowl in there is an the ______________________________
5. field peacocks in there the are ______________________________

Think & Share Pair up with a classmate to play "What's in the box?" Place different items in a box, seal it with tape and ask your partner to guess what is inside. They can only ask questions with **is** and **are** to get clues. For example, "**Are** there beads in the box?"

 ISBN 978-93-5103-601-2

11 Punctuation

Let's Recall

- Signs such as full stops, question marks and exclamation marks help to make the meaning of a sentence clear. They are called **punctuation**.
- We use **capital letters** at the start of a sentence and with special names of people, places, animals and things.
- We use a **full stop** (.) at the end of a statement.
- We use a **question mark** (?) at the end of a question.
- We use an **exclamation mark** (!) at the end of a word, a group of words or a sentence to show strong feeling, such as surprise, happiness, pain, fear or anger.
- Words that show a sudden and strong emotion are called **interjections**. They are followed by exclamation marks, for example, **Ouch!**
- We sometimes join some words together with ' to make a short form. The ' takes the place of the missing letter or letters, for example, ' takes the place of **i** in **he's**.

11.1 Revising punctuation

1. Rewrite each sentence by using **capital letters** and the correct **punctuation** where needed.

   a. Did you hear marie calling us for dinner!

   ____

   b. Mum visits london in december every year.

   ____

   c. Help i am stuck

   ____

2. Fill in each blank with an **interjection** from the box below.

Wow!	Ouch!	Oops!	Help!	Stop!

   a. __________ I broke the plate.

   b. __________ These thorns are sharp.

 ISBN 978-93-5103-601-2

c. ________ Kitty is stuck in the tree! 

d. ________ Your painting is amazing! 

e. ________ Children are not allowed here. 

3. Complete the story below by adding ' where needed.

Today is the kite festival at the city park. Im here with my father and sister, Devina. Were very excited. Dad is excited because hes flying a kite after many years. Devina, however, is the most excited of all. Shes never flown a kite before. Dad is teaching her how to fly one. Theyre really enjoying themselves. Its fun to watch them.

4. Write the **short form** of each underlined word in the blank.

a. <u>You are</u> listening to the radio. ________

b. I think <u>I am</u> coming down with flu. ________

c. Tim does not want to play because <u>he is</u> tired. ________

d. Atul wants to sell his car but <u>it is</u> too old. ________

e. <u>We are</u> going on a holiday next month. ________

f. <u>They are</u> learning how to play the violin. ________

 ISBN 978-93-5103-601-2

11.2 More about short forms

Read the story.

"Today, **you'll** learn about different types of reptiles," says Mrs Brown.

"Tomorrow, **we'll** discuss dinosaurs. Who would like to present a report on them?"

"**I'll** do it, Mrs Brown. My mother is a scientist. **She'll** help me with the facts," says Lyla.

What subject do you think Mrs Brown teaches? Do you enjoy it? Why?

What does Mrs Brown say the students will do today?

What does Mrs Brown say they will do tomorrow?

What will Lyla's mother do?

1. Read the story again. Write the short form of each pair of words below.

   a. you will: ________

   b. we shall: ________

   c. I shall: ________

   d. she will: ________

2. Underline two words in the following sentences that you can write as a short form. Then write the short form in each blank.

   a. Sana thinks it will be cold tomorrow. ________

   b. They will carry the cupboard upstairs. ________

   c. Dad says he will take me to the zoo on Sunday. ________

   d. You will find the keys under the mat at the front door. ________

   e. Priya says she will bring the sketch pens. ________

   f. If we practise regularly, we shall become good football players. ________

When we use the helping verbs **will** and **shall** to talk about things that will happen in the future, we often use the short form **'ll**.

 ISBN 978-93-5103-601-2

Let's Practise

A. Circle the correct **short form** to complete each sentence.

1. Anna says (she'll / he'll) bring the books you need.
2. (They'll / It'll) be time for us to go home soon.
3. Mark thinks (he'll / it'll) pass the test easily.
4. (We'll / You'll) leave the bags where we found them.
5. (They'll / She'll) call us when they are ready.
6. (It'll / You'll) have to do your work yourself.

Remember!
We use **shall** with the pronouns **I** and **we**.

B. Make sentences using the **short forms** of the words given below. The pictures will help you.

1. She will 

____

2. He will 

____

3. We shall 

____

4. They will 

____

5. It will 

____

Think & Share Play the "Short-Form Matching" game. Pair up with a classmate. Make a set of cards with short forms and their full forms. Arrange the cards face down in three rows. Take turns to pick up each card, read the words on it and place it face down again. Each of you has to match the short form to the full form by remembering what is written on each card and turning up the right matching card. The person who makes the most pairs wins the game.

 ISBN 978-93-5103-601-2

11.3 The comma

Read the story.

Jo, Pat, Liam, Andy and Jill visited a factory with their Science teacher.

They saw workers putting together, checking and packing different machines.

A friendly worker told Pat that the machines would go to shops, schools, offices and hospitals.

What kind of things does the factory make? Why do you think so?

Who visited the factory?

What were the workers doing?

Where will the machines go?

1. Fill in each blank with words from the story above.

    a. Names of the children who visited the factory:

    ____

    b. Work that the workers were doing:

    ____

    c. Places the machines will be sent to:

    ____

2. Look at the sentences in the story above. Now add the correct punctuation in the following sentences.

    a. During the summer vacation we are going to Goa Bangalore Delhi and Hyderabad.

    b. We decorated the room with red blue yellow green purple and orange balloons.

    c. Children were hopping skipping jumping and running in the playground.

    d. Please bring a sleeping bag a blanket a water bottle and a jacket to the camp.

The punctuation mark that separates words within a sentence is called the **comma**. We use the comma where we want a pause. We also use it to separate three or more words in a series.

 ISBN 978-93-5103-601-2

Let's Practise

A. Add **commas** where needed in each sentence.

1. I watched the film with Dad Mum Bobby and Anju.

2. We saw eagles parrots and swans during our nature walk.

3. Air water food and shelter are our basic needs.

4. Mrs Brown's garden is blooming with roses jasmines lilies and daffodils.

5. You'll need rice noodles vegetables and sauces to cook a Chinese meal.

B. Make a sentence using the list of things given below, using **commas** where needed.

1. kind helpful friendly

____

2. Mercury Venus Earth Mars

____

3. jogging walking swimming cycling

____

4. squares circles triangles rectangles

____

5. apples apricots plums peaches pears

____

Think & Share Pair up with a partner to set tasks for your classmates. Write a sentence with a list of your classmates' names stating which task they are responsible for. For example, Anna, Binod, Tanmay and Ria will collect library books. You can also set different tasks for one classmate. For example, Tina will collect pens, pencils, rulers and erasers. Remember to use commas.

 ISBN 978-93-5103-601-2

Review 3

1. Underline the **preposition** in each sentence.
   a. Mona jogged around the park.
   b. Grandfather and I walked slowly to the lake.
   c. Our neighbour's dog ran through our garden.
   d. Salim lives across that busy street.
   e. Mum placed a small cushion between two large cushions.
   f. Ameya bought a collar for her pet dog.
   g. There is a rag hanging above the shelf.
   h. I studied an ant through the microscope.
   i. Zia searched the house for her bag.

2. Fill in the blank with a **preposition** from the box below.

before	after	in	at	on	during

   a. Seema's flight landed ________ its arrival time.
   b. Ann's fifth birthday party began ________ one o'clock.
   c. The baker mixed the dough ________ adding water.
   d. Monica will watch a film ________ Sunday.
   e. I asked my friends if they wanted to play cricket ________ recess.
   f. Mohit usually plays basketball ________ the evening.

3. Circle the correct **conjunction** to complete each sentence.
   a. I cannot go outside (though / because) I am sick.
   b. Tom was afraid of dropping the box (so / because) he held it tightly.
   c. Mum kept working (though / so) she was very tired.
   d. Gaurav ate only three biscuits (though / so) he was very hungry.
   e. Hema likes this book (because / though) it is very interesting.
   f. Dad wanted to watch the news, (so / because) I turned on the television.

 ISBN 978-93-5103-601-2

4. Match the sentence parts and join them using **so**, **though** or **because**. Then write the sentences in the blanks below.

Column A	Column B
Maggie learns yoga in the morning	she has gone to the doctor.
I wanted to wake up early	it rained a lot.
I am putting on some sunscreen	I set the alarm on my clock.
The class had a great time at the zoo	it is a sunny day.
Geeta is absent from class	she has little time to prepare her lunch.

a. ______________________________

b. ______________________________

c. ______________________________

d. ______________________________

e. ______________________________

5. Underline the **subject**. Then circle the correct **verb** to complete each sentence.

a. Deserts (is / are) very hot places.

b. I (is participating / am participating) in the race.

c. Dina (is crossing / are crossing) the road.

d. The policeman (was chasing / were chasing) the thief.

e. My sister (was playing / were playing) with her friends.

f. News reporters (are rushing / is rushing) to the site of the accident.

g. Pam (like / likes) tomatoes and carrots in her salad.

h. Geese and swallows (migrate / migrates) to warmer places in winter.

i. You (will be wearing / is wearing) the blue costume.

j. The baboon (is / are) running across the wooden bridge.

6. Use each **subject-verb** pair given below to make a sentence. Remember to use the correct form of the verb.

a. Eagles soars

____

b. The gardener dig

____

c. Librarians helps

____

 ISBN 978-93-5103-601-2

d. My knee hurt

____

e. Glass break

____

f. Tim and Roy paints

____

7. Change the following statements into **questions**.

a. I am making progress.

____

b. There is a solar eclipse today.

____

c. The mayor is holding a meeting at the local park.

____

d. Anita was learning about mammals last week.

____

e. There are strong winds blowing across the desert.

____

f. The teachers were helping the children rehearse their song.

____

8. Underline the **short form** in each sentence. Then write the full form in the blank given.

a. We'll meet at the shop before we go to Rita's party. __________

b. Jogi's friends are sure they'll find an answer to his riddle. __________

c. Dad has called to say he'll be late for the Khans' dinner tonight. __________

d. Grandmother has promised she'll tell us the story of India's independence. __________

e. You'll be able to find your way around the city using the professor's map. __________

f. The gardener's son planted the seed but it'll take some time to grow. __________

9. Write sentences using the following **short forms**.

a. she'll: ____

b. you'll: ____

c. he'll: ____

 ISBN 978-93-5103-601-2

d. they'll: ____________________

e. we'll: ____________________

f. it'll: ____________________

10. Add **commas** where needed in the sentences below.

a. The guests ordered milkshake fruit and toast for breakfast.

b. There are tablespoons teaspoons forks and knives in the top drawer.

c. We use full stops commas exclamation marks and question marks for punctuation.

d. Charles Darwin Albert Einstein Isaac Newton and Stephen Hawking are famous scientists.

e. Asia Africa Europe North America South America Australia and Antarctica are all continents.

f. Debbie packed cardigans hats scarves gloves woollen coats leg warmers and boots for her trip to Europe.

Spot the Error

11. There is a mistake in each sentence. Underline it and rewrite the sentence correctly in the blank below.

a. We took a lot of photos when we went in the zoo.

____

b. There is a bridge around the narrow part of the river.

____

c. Grandmother naps at the afternoon.

____

d. Michael asked for a glass of water though he was thirsty after his run.

____

e. Sam wore a sweater so it wasn't cold outside.

____

f. Farah make beautiful bags and scarves.

____

g. Tanu and Varun eats a lot of sweets.

____

h. This is the best view of the city's skyline?

____

i. My sister's team is confident he'll win the tournament.

____

j. The market stall has jams, pickles chutneys and relishes.

____

 ISBN 978-93-5103-601-2

12 Comprehension

12.1 Concluding

As you read, you should think carefully about the facts and details in the text and decide what they actually mean. This is called concluding.

Take Note
A fable
- is a short story with a moral that teaches us about right and wrong behaviour.
- often has animals or non-living objects as characters.
- usually shows the characters facing a problem or test.

Read the fable.

The Ant and the Dove

One day, a thirsty ant went to a stream for a drink. As she reached down to take a sip, she fell in and was swept away by the water. "Help!" she cried. A dove sitting on a tree by the stream heard her cry. He plucked a leaf and dropped it into the stream. The ant scrambled onto the leaf and floated to safety. She thanked the dove for his kindness.

A few days later, the ant saw a hunter setting a trap for the dove. The dove did not see the hunter. The ant hurried towards the hunter and bit him on his leg. He cried out in pain. The cry alerted the dove, and he quickly flew off into the sky.

Think!
In order to conclude, you
- understand what you are making a conclusion about.
- find the facts and details from the text.
- decide what exactly the facts and details mean.

Answer the questions.

1. What is the moral of the fable?

   a. Be kind to people and they'll be kind to you. b. Be careful when you go near a stream.

2. You can conclude that the dove was kind-hearted because

   a. he gave the ant a leaf to eat. b. he saved the ant from drowning.

3. Why did the hunter cry out?

   a. He was in pain. b. The dove flew away. c. He fell down.

4. What does the word **scrambled** mean? Tick the correct answer.

   a. to swim fast b. to move or climb in a hurry c. to float

5. Fill in the blanks with the correct form of the verb given in the brackets.

   a. An ant ____ (go) to a stream. b. She ____ (fall) into the water.

 ISBN 978-93-5103-601-2

Let's Practise

The Thirsty Crow

One hot summer day, a crow flew all over the city in search of water. He did not find even a drop. Soon, he became weak with thirst. He felt sure he would die.

Suddenly, the crow saw a pitcher in a garden. He hopped close to the pitcher and peered inside. He was delighted to see a little water at the bottom. However, when he put his beak into the mouth of the pitcher, he found that he could not reach the water.

Just then the crow had an idea. He picked up a pebble with his beak and dropped it into the pitcher. He took another pebble and dropped it in. He dropped many pebbles into the pitcher in this way. The water rose up. He finally had water to drink.

Answer the questions.

A. What is the moral of the fable?

1. Hopping is better than flying.
2. Keep trying till you achieve your goal.
3. It is better to be clever than strong.

B. The crow hopped to the pitcher because

1. he was too weak to fly.
2. he liked hopping.
3. he was scared of the pitcher.

C. We can conclude that the crow was clever because

1. he found water to drink.
2. he could pick up pebbles with his beak.
3. he found a way to reach the water in the pitcher.

D. What does the word **peered** mean? Tick the correct answer.

1. jumped 2. sniffed 3. looked

E. Circle the correct collective noun to complete each sentence.

1. Ada saw a (colony / bouquet) of ants in her backyard.
2. A (murder / bundle) of crows flew over the roof.
3. The captain released a (herd / flight) of doves during the ceremony.

 ISBN 978-93-5103-601-2

12.2 Predicting

As you read, it is important to understand what is happening in a story and try to think what might happen next. This is called predicting.

Take Note

A playscript
- reports a conversation or dialogue between people, animals or things.
- describes the scene where the action takes place.
- is written in order to be performed on the stage by actors.

Read the playscript.

Aditya: Why are you carrying that costume?

Gauri: I am participating in the school play this year.

Aditya: That's great news! What is the play about?

Gauri: It's about a girl who bravely defends her country against an evil wizard.

Aditya: What role are you playing?

Gauri: I play the evil wizard.

Aditya: That sounds very interesting.

Gauri: It is. I have never played an evil character before.

Aditya: Did you face any hurdles?

Gauri: A few. It was difficult to get the voice right at first. I found it hard to sound like a man.

Aditya: And now?

Gauri: Now I scare the people who are watching us rehearse on stage!

Think!

In order to predict, you
- find information related to the question.
- think about the information and ask yourself, "What is the writer suggesting might happen?"

Answer the questions.

1. Where will Gauri probably go after talking to Aditya?
   a. the science laboratory
   b. the swimming pool
   c. the school auditorium

 ISBN 978-93-5103-601-2

2. What do you think would happen if Gauri were not able to sound like a man for the play?

   a. She would ask the director to get someone else to play the role.

   b. She would ask for some more time to practise and get the voice right.

   c. She would ask the director for another role in the play.

3. If Gauri gets a chance to play a difficult character in the next play, what do you think she will do?

   a. She will refuse to take part.

   b. She will ask Aditya to do the role.

   c. She will accept the challenge and practise hard to play the role well.

4. How do you think Gauri will feel after taking part in the play?

   a. scared   b. confident   c. evil

5. What does the word **hurdles** mean? Tick the correct answer.

   a. fences   b. difficulties   c. evil people

6. Change the following statements into questions.

   a. My teacher is directing the school play this year.

   ____

   b. The costumes are ready.

   ____

   c. It was difficult to get the voice right at first.

   ____

7. Change the tense of the underlined verb as indicated in the brackets.

   Example The girl defends her country against an evil wizard. (simple future tense)

   The girl will defend her country against an evil wizard.

   a. I play the evil wizard. (simple past tense)

   ____

   b. I found it hard to sound like a man. (simple present tense)

   ____

   c. I scare the people who are watching us rehearse. (present continuous tense)

   ____

 ISBN 978-93-5103-601-2

Let's Practise

Ayesha: Mum, I'm home!

Mrs Roy: How was school? How was your spelling test?

Ayesha: School was fun. I did very well in the test, though I was so nervous this morning!

Mrs Roy: If you prepare in advance, you'll feel more confident next time.

Ayesha: Yes, that's my plan for next week's test. What have you made? It smells so good.

Mrs Roy: I'm baking brownies for the team. I'll take these to the office tomorrow.

Ayesha: Wow! May I have one, please?

Mrs Roy: Why don't you have one after dinner?

Ayesha: Please, Mum! I don't want to wait.

Mrs Roy: Okay! Just one, then.

Answer the questions.

A. Where do you think this dialogue is taking place?

1. in the kitchen 2. in Ayesha's room 3. at the front door

B. How do you think Ayesha will feel when she takes the test next week?

1. scared 2. confident 3. excited

C. The next time Mrs Roy's team asks her to bake brownies, she will

1. tell them she doesn't have the time.
2. bake a few extra so that Ayesha gets some too.
3. bake just enough brownies for the team.

D. What does **in advance** mean? Tick the correct answer.

1. for a week 2. for a longer time 3. ahead of time

 ISBN 978-93-5103-601-2

12.3 Summarising

When you talk about what you have read, you need to put together the main points in as few words as possible. This is called summarising.

Read the report.

Paper, Paper Everywhere!

Paper is a very useful material. It is all around us. We use it daily for a variety of things in many different ways. We use it to make newspapers, tissues, writing paper, cards, paper bags, glossy magazines and lots of other things.

Paper comes from wood, which we get from trees. Trees are cut and the wood is taken to factories. This wood then goes through a process in the factories. It is heated and mixed with water and chemicals. This makes a thick paste called wood pulp that is poured out in flat layers. All the water is squeezed out and the wood pulp is dried in the form of sheets. Chemicals are added to change the colour and appearance of the sheets as needed.

Paper is essential for us. In how many ways have you used paper today?

Take Note

A report
- gives information or facts about things, people, animals or happenings.
- begins with a general statement that introduces the topic.
- gives facts about the topic in a logical manner.
- ends with a concluding statement or question.

Answer the questions.

1. Which sentence would you leave out of a summary of how paper is useful to us?
   a. We use paper to write reports on.
   b. Paper can be glossy.
   c. Paper is used to make cards.
2. Summarise what is described in the second paragraph.

   ____

   ____
3. Read the report carefully and complete the sentence.

   It is hard to imagine life without paper because ______________

   ____
4. What does the word **essential** mean? Tick the correct answer.

   a. necessary   b. special   c. dangerous
5. Find four prepositions in the report and write them in the blanks below.

   a. ________ b. ________ c. ________ d. ________

Think!

When you summarise, you
- look carefully at the information in the text.
- decide on what is important and how it is connected.
- leave out any unnecessary information.

 ISBN 978-93-5103-601-2

Let's Practise

Brilliant Bees!

Honeybees are nature's example of teamwork. Thousands of honeybees live together in a beehive. They visit hundreds of flowers a day in spring and summer. They collect nectar from the flowers. They take the nectar to their hive to make honey.

First, they make sheets of wax called honeycombs inside the beehive. The honeycombs have small cells in which the bees put the nectar. They dry the nectar by fanning it with their wings. The nectar becomes thick and turns into honey. Through winter, the bees live on the stored honey. They feed it to the young bees.

All the bees in the hive work together for the good of the hive. The queen bee lays eggs. Worker bees collect food. They show excellent teamwork.

Answer the questions.

A. What is the report about?

1. Beehives
2. Teamwork among honeybees
3. Honey

B. Write a sentence that summarises how honey is made.

____

____

C. Tick the sentence that best summarises why honeycombs are important for honeybees.

1. Honeycombs have small cells.
2. Honeybees make honeycombs.
3. Honey is stored in honeycombs.

D. Which of the following words can replace the word **fanning**?

1. folding   2. cooling   3. flying

E. Circle the correct verb to complete each sentence.

1. Honeybees (collect / collects) nectar from flowers.
2. Bees (dries / dry) nectar by fanning it with their wings.
3. The queen bee (lay / lays) eggs.

 ISBN 978-93-5103-601-2

12.4 Fact or opinion

When you read, you should try to understand the difference between what is true (fact) and what someone believes is true (opinion). This is called distinguishing between fact and opinion.

Read the diary entry.

Take Note

A diary entry
- is a personal note that describes events, feelings and experiences.
- uses the pronoun **I**.
- is usually written in the past tense.

Wednesday, 2 March 2016

Dear Diary,

Today was a special day! I lost my first milk tooth. It had been wiggly for such a long time, I was beginning to think it would never fall out. But finally, it did! It happened at lunchtime in school. I was so excited, I ran to tell my friends. Meeta and Tasha have both lost three teeth each. Now I am part of the "funny smile" club in class! Tonight I will put my tooth under my pillow. Meeta told me the tooth fairy comes at night and takes it away. I believe she will leave a small gift for me. I can't wait for tomorrow morning!

Alisha

Think!

To find out if a statement is a fact or an opinion, you
- check if the statement can be proved to be true. If it can be proved, it is a fact.
- check if the statement shows what someone thinks or believes. If it cannot be proved to be true, it is an opinion.

Answer the questions.

1. What is the diary entry about?
   a. The day Alisha lost her first milk tooth
   b. Alisha's funny smile
   c. The tooth fairy

 ISBN 978-93-5103-601-2

2. Read this sentence.

"Meeta and Tasha have both lost three teeth each."

a. Is it a fact or an opinion? ______________________________

b. Why do you think so? ______________________________

3. Tick the sentence(s) that are facts.

a. Alisha lost her first milk tooth. ☐

b. The tooth fairy will leave a small gift for Alisha. ☐

c. The tooth fell out at lunchtime in school. ☐

4. Tick the sentence(s) that are opinions.

a. It is exciting to have a wiggly tooth. ☐

b. The tooth was wiggly for a long time. ☐

c. Alisha became a part of the "funny smile" club. ☐

5. Underline the word that tells you that each sentence is an opinion.

a. I was beginning to think it would never fall.

b. I believe she will leave a small gift for me.

6. Add **'s** or **'** to show belonging. Rewrite each sentence in the blank below.

a. The tooth belonging to Alisha was wiggly.

____

b. The smiles belonging to Meeta and Tasha were funny.

____

c. Alisha was looking forward to receiving the gift of the tooth fairy.

____

7. Underline the adjectives in the sentences below. Then rewrite each sentence using a different adjective.

a. Today was a special day!

____

b. I will put my tooth under my soft pillow.

____

c. I drank hot milk at lunch today.

____

d. Meeta carries a steel lunchbox to school.

____

 ISBN 978-93-5103-601-2

Let's Practise

Monday, 27 July 2016

Dear Diary,

Mum made a new rule today – no tidying up! I couldn't believe it. What a super rule! In the morning, I left the room with the bedclothes thrown in a pile. My pyjamas lay on the floor. I ate breakfast in my room, and I didn't put my plate and bowl away before I left for school. It felt a bit strange, but I didn't mind. I had a great day at school, but when I returned everything was still a mess. I tripped on the bedclothes, and I couldn't find my chessboard in all the clutter. It felt like a bad dream. What a terrible rule!

Rahul

Answer the questions.

A. What is Rahul's diary entry about?
   1. The importance of tidying up
   2. Rahul's dislike of tidying up
   3. Rahul's room

B. Tick the statement(s) that are facts.
   1. Mum made a new rule today.
   2. It was a super rule!
   3. Rahul left the room with his clothes thrown in a pile.

C. When did Rahul change his opinion about Mum's rule?
   1. when he saw his messy room in the afternoon
   2. when Mum explained why tidying up is important

D. What does the word **clutter** mean? Tick the correct answer.
   1. cupboard   2. bedclothes   3. mess

E. Join each pair of sentences with the conjunction given in the brackets.
   1. I left my clothes on the floor. I couldn't find my chessboard. (so)

      ____

   2. I tripped. I had left my bedclothes on the floor. (because)

      ____

 ISBN 978-93-5103-601-2

13 Composition

13.1 Paragraph

A paragraph is a group of sentences that describes or explains an idea.

Take Note
A paragraph
- has a title or heading.
- begins with a topic sentence and ends with a concluding sentence.
- contains topic words that relate to the topic.

Songkran — **Title**

The new year in Thailand is called Songkran. It comes at the start of summer. People celebrate with their family and friends over three days on **13**, **14** and **15 April**. Songkran is celebrated as a **water festival**. People spray water on each other to wash off the bad luck of the past year. Some people use buckets and garden hoses to drench others. Some even use elephants to spray water on passers-by! Others cover friends and family in **chalk**. **Monks and devotees wash statues** of Lord Buddha. People **visit older family members** and pour fragrant water over their hands as a sign of respect. They get rid of old and useless things and make new resolutions. **Songkran is an occasion for everyone to greet each other, celebrate and wish for good times in the new year.**

Topic sentence
Start with a topic sentence that says what the paragraph is about.

Topic words
Give more details about the topic by using topic words.

Concluding sentence
Make a final comment on the main idea of the paragraph.

 ISBN 978-93-5103-601-2

Let's Practise

A. Use the outline given below to write a paragraph. Remember to give a title to your paragraph.

The Internet – big network – links computers all across the world – acts like a giant notice board – displays news and information – learn about various subjects – share our learning – quick and easy way to connect with family and friends everywhere – in a few seconds – respond right away – very useful

 ISBN 978-93-5103-601-2

1. What is the topic sentence of your paragraph?

____

2. Write the topic words below.

____

____

3. What is the concluding sentence of your paragraph?

____

B. Use the outline given below to write a paragraph. Remember to give a title to your paragraph.

Many people keep pets – bring joy to our lives – cats and dogs most common pets – cats are good company – not as playful as dogs – dogs are very loving – can help heal diseases – take away our loneliness – we should take good care of our pets – depend on us for everything

____

____

____

____

____

____

____

____

____

____

____

____

____

____

 ISBN 978-93-5103-601-2

13.2 Informal letter

An informal letter is a personal note to a friend or relative.

Take Note
An informal letter has three main parts:
1. Greeting
2. Body
3. Signature

5 Waterloo Quay
Edinburgh
Scotland

Address
Address on the left

21 February 2016

Date
Date below the address

Dear Raj,

Greeting
Use the first name.

How are you and your family? It must be summer in New Delhi now. Is it really hot?

I wish I could visit India in summer. Here in Edinburgh, it is very cold. I wear three layers of clothes and thick woollen socks in this weather.

I have two best friends here. They are Peter and Sarah. We are in the same class. We like going ice skating together at the weekend.

Do you get a lot of homework? We don't get any, but we have to do a lot of projects. Tell me all about your school and friends.

Body
Write all the things you want to talk about in one or more paragraphs.

Best wishes,

Harry

Signature
End with a final greeting and your first name.

 ISBN 978-93-5103-601-2

Let's Practise

A. Raj writes a reply to his friend Harry in Scotland. Complete his letter with the words given in the box below.

the monsoon to arrive	for your letter	Raj	Harry
when it is cooler	ten glasses of lemonade	Your friend,	
a project about the monsoon	like cycling in the park together		
from the heat	5 March 2016		

A/21 Rajender Nagar
New Delhi

____

Dear ______________,

How are you? Thank you ______________________.

It is really hot and humid here. I must have had ______________________ to cool down today! We are all waiting for ______________________. The rains will bring a lot of relief ______________________.

I have two best friends too. They are Sanju and Kabir. We are also in the same class. We ______________________. We go in the evening ______________________.

Yes, I get heaps of homework, but right now we are preparing for our exams. I am working on ______________________.

It would be wonderful if you could visit us soon.

____

____

 ISBN 978-93-5103-601-2

B. Sonia writes a letter to her cousin Amna describing an interesting book she read in her school library. Complete her letter.

____

____

28 June 2016

____

How are you? ____

I must tell you about ____________________________________

____

____

____

____

____

I am looking forward to ____________________________________.

Love,

____

 ISBN 978-93-5103-601-2

Review 4

1. Read the fable.

The Donkey and its Shadow

One day, a donkey and its owner were walking down the road. A passing traveller asked if he could hire the donkey to carry his bags. The donkey's owner agreed for five silver coins. The traveller loaded his bags on the donkey and they set off. Soon they were very tired. They decided to rest, but the only shade they could find was in the donkey's shadow.

Both men tried to sit in the shadow of the donkey, but there was not enough space. They began to quarrel. The traveller said he should rest in the donkey's shadow because he had paid for it. The owner disagreed and said the traveller had only paid for the donkey to carry his bags, not to sit in its shadow. On and on they argued. While they were arguing, the donkey galloped away. Now they had no donkey, no bags and no shade!

a. What is the moral of the fable?
   i. When we argue over small matters, we lose what really matters.
   ii. It is not wise to argue in the afternoon.
   iii. Donkeys may gallop away if they are not watched.

b. Why did the traveller want the donkey to carry his bags?
   i. He wanted the donkey to do some work.
   ii. The bags were heavy.
   iii. He wanted to give money to the owner.

c. You can conclude that it was a hot day because
   i. the donkey galloped away.
   ii. the donkey's owner took five silver coins from the traveller.
   iii. both men fought about who should sit in the donkey's shadow.

d. What does **quarrel** mean?
   i. argue
   ii. hit
   iii. talk loudly

 ISBN 978-93-5103-601-2

2. Read the playscript.

Jenny is reading a book while Tim is practising his guitar.

Jenny: Tim, why are you playing the guitar just now?

Tim: I have a test tomorrow morning. I must practise tonight.

Jenny: It's too noisy. I can't concentrate.

Tim: I'm not that bad!

Jenny: I didn't say that. I just need a quiet place to read.

Tim: Sorry, but I can't go outside to practise. It's too cold and windy!

Jenny: True! And the neighbours might complain about the noise.

Tim: I have an idea!

Jenny: What is it?

Tim: I will get you my headphones. You can put them on to block out the sound.

Jenny: Brilliant!

a. What is Jenny complaining about?

   i. the noise from the guitar
   ii. the neighbours
   iii. reading

b. What do you think might happen if Tim practised outdoors?
   i. The cold wind might blow the guitar away.
   ii. The cold wind might blow Tim away.
   iii. Tim might catch a cold.

c. How do you think Tim feels once Jenny accepts his suggestion?
   i. happy
   ii. unhappy
   iii. doubtful

d. What does **concentrate** mean?
   i. pay close attention
   ii. read
   iii. play the guitar

e. Write a noun to match each adjective given below.

   i. cold ________ ii. noisy ________ iii. quiet ________

 ISBN 978-93-5103-601-2

3. Read the report.

Clever Crocodiles

Crocodiles are ferocious animals that usually live in and near lakes and rivers. They mostly feed on fish, birds and other animals. All these animals are their prey.

Crocodiles are usually brown, grey or green with black spots. This makes them look like logs of wood floating in the water. Crocodiles are very clever hunters. They float just below the water's surface. Their eyes, ears and nostrils are raised above the water, so they can easily see, hear and smell their prey. The prey cannot see them because most of their body is hidden. They attack their prey suddenly and swiftly.

a. What is the article about?

 i. How crocodiles hunt

 ii. How crocodiles swim

 iii. How animals float

b. Which sentence gives a good summary of the second paragraph?

 i. Crocodiles are ferocious animals.

 ii. Crocodiles have a clever way of hunting.

 iii. Crocodiles are ferocious and colourful.

c. Most prey cannot escape a crocodile because

 i. it moves so fast that the prey does not have time to run away.

 ii. the prey cannot see as well as the crocodile can.

d. Underline the prepositions in the second paragraph. Then write sentences using any two prepositions.

____

____

Spot the Error

e. There is a mistake in each sentence. Underline it and rewrite the sentence correctly in the blank below.

 i. Crocodiles are usually living in lakes and rivers.

____

 ii. Crocodiles feeds on fish, birds and other animals.

____

 iii. Crocodiles attack their pray suddenly and swiftly.

____

 iv. Crocodiles are the more ferocious of all animals.

____

 ISBN 978-93-5103-601-2

4. Write a paragraph on any one topic given below. Remember to write the title first.

   a. Fruit and vegetables

   b. Majestic lions

   c. The importance of exercise

5. Write a letter to your cousin about your favourite hobby.

 ISBN 978-93-5103-601-2

Word Power

Synonyms

Synonyms are words that mean the same or nearly the same.

Fill in the table with suitable synonyms from the box below.

meet	protect	excellent	frighten	clutter	gather
shiny	press	weird	middle	necessary	fearless

a.	brave		g.	mess	
b.	centre		h.	scare	
c.	collect		i.	squeeze	
d.	defend		j.	strange	
e.	essential		k.	very good	
f.	glossy		l.	visit	

Antonyms

Antonyms are words that are opposite in meaning.

Match the words in the boxes to form pairs of antonyms. Then write the pairs in the blanks below.

float	nervous	work
bottom	useful	lose
interesting	thick	smile
evil	dry	sleep

confident	boring	good
rest	wet	wake
sink	top	thin
find	frown	useless

_______________ _______________ _______________

_______________ _______________ _______________

_______________ _______________ _______________

_______________ _______________ _______________

 ISBN 978-93-5103-601-2

Words that sound the same

Some words sound the same, but have different spellings and meanings.

Complete each word with the help of the picture. Then match the columns to form pairs of words that sound the same.

a.  p _ n _ •		• i.  st _ _ l
b.  to _ _ •		• ii.  w _ _ g _ t
c.  w _ _ t •		• iii.  p _ _ n
d.  st _ _ l •		• iv.  t _ w _ d

Words that have the same spelling

Some words have the same spelling, but they sound different and have different meanings.

Fill in each set of blanks with words from the box below. Then match each pair of sentences to the correct meanings.

wound	live	bow	wind

a. The ________ is blowing hard. Grandfather has to ________ the clock every day. •	• i. tied around (rhymes with **found**) injury (rhymes with **spooned**)
b. Lions ________ in dens. The cricket match will be telecast ________. •	• ii. moving air (rhymes with **pinned**) turn (rhymes with **find**)
c. The thread was ________ around a reel. The ________ on my arm has healed. •	• iii. bend as a sign of respect (rhymes with **cow**) a decorative knot (rhymes with **so**)
d. Alka took a ________ after her performance. Hina tied a ________ in her hair. •	• iv. exist (rhymes with **give**) as it is happening (rhymes with **hive**)

 ISBN 978-93-5103-601-2

Similes

A simile is a group of words that compares two things using the words **like** or **as**.

1. Fill in each blank with the correct noun. The picture will help you. Then match the columns to complete the similes.

a. as hard as a •	• i.		________
b. as blind as a •	• ii.		________
c. as sharp as a •	• iii.		________
d. as dry as a •	• iv.		________
e. as light as a •	• v.		________
f. as slow as a •	• vi.		________

2. Now use the similes above to complete each sentence.

   a. This silk scarf is ____________________.

   b. This train is ____________________.

   c. Without his glasses, my uncle is ____________________.

   d. Ouch! This hairpin is ____________________.

   e. I was surprised to find the cake was ____________________.

   f. I went to the well to get some water but it was ____________________.

3. Match each group of words to the correct simile to complete the sentence.

a. When Mandy saw the snake, she ran •	• i. like a clown.
b. Sandy always fools around and acts •	• ii. like a monkey.
c. After the race, Vivek fell on his bed •	• iii. like a glove.
d. In summer, our flat heats up •	• iv. like the wind.
e. Alisha can climb over walls •	• v. like an oven.
f. The dress fit Asha •	• vi. like a sack of potatoes.

 ISBN 978-93-5103-601-2